W9-AZJ-699

$10–
7/6

The Shaker Image

The road to Hancock Shaker Village.

THE SHAKER IMAGE

Elmer R. Pearson, PICTURE EDITOR

Julia Neal, THE SHAKERS, AS THEY SAW
THEMSELVES AND AS OTHERS SAW THEM

WITH A PREFACE BY *Walter Muir Whitehill*
AND CAPTIONS BY *Amy Bess Miller* AND *John H. Ott*

New York Graphic Society
BOSTON, MASSACHUSETTS
IN COLLABORATION WITH

Shaker Community, Inc.
HANCOCK, MASSACHUSETTS

International Standard Book Number 0-8212-0539-0
Library of Congress Catalog Card Number 73-89954

Copyright © 1974 by Shaker Community, Inc.

First published 1974 by New York Graphic Society Ltd.

All rights reserved. No portion of the contents of this
book may be reproduced or used in any form or by any means
without written permission of the publishers.
Designed by Peter Oldenburg

Manufactured in the United States of America

THIS BOOK IS DEDICATED TO THE
THOUSANDS OF SHAKERS
WHO SINCE 1774 HAVE LABORED
TO IMPROVE THE QUALITY OF LIFE AND
TO FOLLOW MOTHER ANN'S DICTATE:
Put your hands to work and your hearts to God.

Shakerism presents a system of faith
and a mode of life, which during the
past century has solved social and
religious problems and successfully
established practical brotherhoods of
industry, besides freeing women from
inequality and injustice.

—Eldresses Anna White
and Leila S. Taylor, 1904

ACKNOWLEDGMENTS

We wish to express our gratitude to the many friends of the Shakers whose knowledge of Shaker history has made this book possible. Through their generosity and interest, photographs never before published will be enjoyed and studied.

We are indebted specifically to the Shaker societies at Canterbury, New Hampshire, and Sabbathday Lake, Maine; Mrs. Curry Hall, director of Shakertown at South Union, Kentucky; William Henry Harrison, director of The Fruitlands Museum, Harvard, Massachusetts; Theodore E. Johnson, director of The Shaker Library, Sabbathday Lake, Maine; Robert F. W. Meader, director of The Shaker Museum, Old Chatham, New York; Kermit Pike, librarian of The Western Reserve Historical Society, Cleveland, Ohio; James C. Thomas, director of Shakertown, Pleasant Hill, Kentucky; Charles Thompson, director of The Shaker Museum, Canterbury, New Hampshire; John Watson, director of The New York State Historical Society, Rotterdam, New York; and Mrs. Julius Zieget.

In particular, we would like to pay tribute to Elmer R. Pearson, whose expertise, knowledge, and feeling for perfection have so wonderfully illuminated the Shaker story.

AMY BESS MILLER, President

JOHN H. OTT, Director

Shaker Community, Inc., Hancock, Massachusetts

Contents

Hancock Shaker Village

IN THE BERKSHIRE HILLS of western Massachusetts a unique and historic rural settlement was brought to life in 1961.

Hancock Shaker Village, "The City of Peace," a home of the Believers founded in 1790, was closed when the last two Shaker sisters left it to reside elsewhere. Public-spirited citizens from near and far accepted responsibility for restoring the Village and preserving it and the values it represented.

Shaker Community, Inc., was formed in August 1960 for non-profit educational purposes, and the lovely old Village passed directly from Shaker to non-Shaker hands.

At the time of the transfer, Eldress Emma B. King, of Canterbury, New Hampshire, the head of the United Society of Believers, stated, in reference to the properties of discontinued Shaker societies:

> The Parent Ministry has always been especially anxious that these lands and buildings be devoted to some use which is charitable or educational and of benefit to the community. . . . It is therefore a satisfaction and a joy to us that the group which will now assume these properties [at Hancock] will use them for the preservation of the Shaker traditions.

The Village comprises twenty buildings on 1,000 acres of land. Fourteen buildings—among them the dwelling house, the round barn, and the meeting house—have been restored and furnished. Six more, including the schoolhouse, await restoration. Pupils in elementary and high schools, and college and graduate-school students and teachers, come to study how the Shakers lived. In thirteen summers, over 350,000 people have found refreshment and education at Hancock Shaker Village.

> We believed we were debtors to God in relation to Each other, and all men, to improve our time and Talents in this Life, in that manner in which we might be most useful.
>
> —Shaker covenant, 1795

9

WALTER MUIR WHITEHILL

Preface

More than fifty years ago, when I was in my teens, I first heard of the Shakers when my mother bought a copy of *Gleanings from Old Shaker Journals*, which had been compiled by Miss Clara Endicott Sears and published by Houghton Mifflin Company in 1916. Miss Sears, who was born in 1863 and died in 1960, was a Boston lady of property and leisure who had built for herself a house on the crest of Prospect Hill in Harvard, Massachusetts, from which one could look across the Nashaway Valley towards Mount Wachusett. Although she was as unencumbered by formal education as most Boston ladies of her generation, Miss Sears had compensating gifts of imagination and energy that led her not only to appreciate the natural beauty and historical implications of her surroundings, but also to do something positive and constructive about them. Thus in 1914 she bought and restored "Fruitlands," a derelict farmhouse lower down Prospect Hill from her house, because it had been the scene in 1843 of the attempt by Bronson Alcott and other high-minded and impractical Transcendentalists to create a "New Eden." Miss Sears's action sprang from her intuitive conviction that "if for a time it had borne the semblance of a New Eden, then that time must be honored, and not forgotten." Having assembled furniture, portraits, and manuscripts of the Transcendentalists who had briefly inhabited the house, Miss Sears opened Fruitlands to visitors in the summer months. In 1915 she compiled a book for Houghton Mifflin entitled *Bronson Alcott's Fruitlands*, in the introduction to which she wrote:

> If that history was full of pathos, if the great experiment enacted beneath its roof proved a failure, the failure was only in the means of expression and not in the idea which inspired it. Humanity must ever reach out towards a New Eden. Succeeding generations smile at the crude attempts, and forthwith make their own blunders, but each attempt, however seemingly unsuccessful, must of necessity contain a germ of spiritual beauty which will bear fruit.

With such a turn of mind, it was inevitable that Miss Sears should be attracted to the dwindling membership of the Shaker community established in 1793 within the town of Harvard. This town had been from 1781 to 1783 the center of the missionary labors in New England of Mother Ann Lee and the scene of some of the bitter persecutions of the missionaries of the infant society of Shakers. A decade after Mother Ann and her followers had been driven out of Harvard, a Shaker community was established there which during the nineteenth century reached a maximum membership of two hundred Believers. In the twentieth century, its numbers steadily shrank, and the community was dissolved in 1918. Miss Sears often visited the last of the Shaker eldresses, and through their friendship gained access to the records from which she compiled *Gleanings from Old Shaker Journals.* When the community came to an end she bought from the deserted Shaker Village a 1794 wooden house and moved it to her own property, resettling it on the hill a little above Fruitlands. This building was opened to exhibit a collection that she had formed illustrative of Shaker life and industries, as a memorial to the extinct community. These personal ventures in historic preservation were made formal in 1930 when Miss Sears incorporated The Fruitlands Museums, to which she subsequently added brick buildings housing collections dealing with the local Indians and with nineteenth-century painting. On her death in 1960 she bequeathed to a board of trustees funds to assure the continued operation of these museums, which recall different but related aspects of the local past.

In the 1920's when Shakers were a fast-disappearing sect, seemingly remote from the current of American life, it would have surprised everyone—even the ever-hopeful Miss Sears—to know the number of American museums that would soon be seeking Shaker artifacts, and to realize that in 1974 the Smithsonian Institution would fill the ground floor of its Renwick Gallery in Washington, diagonally across Pennsylvania Avenue from the White House, with an exhibition of Shaker furniture and objects in commemoration of the bicentenary of the arrival on this continent of Mother Ann Lee and her little band of followers.

Yet in the past fifty years interest in everything having to do with the Shakers has steadily grown, thanks in large part to the collecting, study, and writing of the late Dr. Edward Deming Andrews and his wife Faith. Their work first came to wide general attention in 1937 when the Yale University Press published their *Shaker Furniture, The Craftsmanship of an American Communal Sect,* a book for which Carl Purington Rollins, Printer to the University, provided a format worthy of the simple, lean elegance of the subject. It was through Carl and Margaret Rollins that I first came to know of the work of Dr. and Mrs. Andrews, and later, in 1960, of the effort of Mrs.

Lawrence K. Miller, of Pittsfield, to preserve the Shaker buildings at Hancock, Massachusetts. This community, organized in 1790, was dissolved 170 years later. Its buildings and surroundings were in imminent danger when Mrs. Miller and a group of sympathetic neighbors and friends created Shaker Community, Inc., a non-profit organization, to buy the site and operate it as a public museum. Dr. Andrews became its first curator, and much of his collection has found its permanent home there.

Over the past fourteen years I have watched with admiration the development of the Hancock scene—the consolidation and restoration of the buildings, especially the remarkable great stone circular barn, the moving of a meeting house from Shirley to replace one destroyed in 1938, and the preservation of a singularly beautiful rural landscape. Although my personal taste is more congenial to Bernini, Boucher, and Byzantium—simply to stay within the second letter of the alphabet—than to the functional austerities of the Shakers, I so admire what Shaker Community, Inc., has accomplished at Hancock that I am happy to be associated with it in any way possible. In 1970 I wrote a brief appreciation of the Shakers to introduce Mrs. Miller's *The Best of Shaker Cooking*. It is a pleasure now to introduce this remarkable collection of photographs of Shaker life whose publication Mrs. Miller has inspired.

These views, which cover the years from about 1860 to about 1925, depict a world that in its details will be almost unrecognizable to many Americans of 1974. There is an inevitable pathos in the disintegration of all "New Edens," but as Miss Sears pointed out while writing of Bronson Alcott nearly sixty years ago, "The failure was only in the means of expression and not in the ideal which inspired it." We are unlikely to see the revival of scenes like those depicted in the pages that follow. Indeed Janet Malcolm, writing on "The Spirit of Shaker Design" in the Smithsonian's Shaker Bicentenary catalogue, contrasts the sordid squalor of present-day communes with the spotless fresh brightness of Shaker communities. But the order and decorum, the superb craftsmanship, and the industry of the Shakers, together with their genius for doing even the simplest and most humdrum thing well, are ideals that could be emulated by Americans in the years ahead.

WALTER MUIR WHITEHILL, author, editor, and teacher, was director and librarian of the Boston Athenaeum from 1946 until his retirement in 1973.

1 The earliest photograph in this book, an ambrotype made about 1860.

2 A photograph of three Shaker sisters and a friend, made about 1925 at Hancock, Massachusetts.

ELMER R. PEARSON

A Word on the Photographs

This book of photographs is unique in that no comprehensive collection of contemporary photographs of the Shakers has ever before been published. The pictures reproduced here have been collected from museums, libraries, private collections, and from Shaker family albums.

I have found that students in the arts on all levels find the Shakers fascinating, perhaps because their life and their art were one and the same thing. My wish to use slides, drawings, and actual objects as much as possible in teaching led me into recording the remaining Shakers buildings and objects. While I was photographing these buildings and living in them from time to time, I could not help wondering what day-to-day life was like when the Shakers were there. And I have found that the Shaker sisters who are still living remembered things from the old photographs that could not be uncovered in any other way.

We have a wealth of written material describing the Shakers' early life, written by visitors, Shaker apostates, and the Shakers themselves, but we have no visual images depicting them in the earliest years of their existence.

The earliest photograph in this book is an ambrotype made around 1860, when the Shaker movement had reached its height (figure 1).

One of the latest, depicting three Shaker sisters—one of them holding a box camera—and a visitor, was made by today's roll-film process at Hancock, Massachusetts, in 1925 (figure 2). By that time the Shakers' way of life had changed so much that in most photographs of them after about 1920 they scarcely resemble the early Believers, and indeed these late photographs seem very much like the photographs taken of the outside world. While they contain invaluable information concerning structures that no longer exist, they are not included in this book.

On account of the Shakers' adherence to celibacy, the sect could stay alive

15

only by winning converts. To help achieve this aim, the Shakers began writing for publication early in their history and continued to do so throughout the 1800's. In addition to countless published books, there also exist hundreds of private diaries and journals which extensively chronicle the progressive changes in their beliefs and attitudes.

The Millennial Laws which governed Shaker life in the early years prohibited the display of images on the walls of most rooms. In the Section, Orders concerning Furniture in Retiring Rooms, the Laws direct that, "No maps, Charts, Pictures nor paintings, should ever be hung up in retiring rooms; and no pictures paintings or likenesses, as Deguerotypes etc. set in frames, or otherwise should ever be kept by Believers. Modest advertisements may be put up in the trustees office when necessary." [1]

Thus, with the exception of the well-known inspirational drawings, which were made in the 1840's and 1850's, no known early Shaker drawings exist. Printed representations of the Shakers—singing, dancing, or in their homes —were always made by outsiders. Most of them were made after the introduction of photography, the early wood and later steel engravings being copied from photographs.

In spite of the large amount of writing done by the Shakers, there is no precise indication of when they began to accept the pictorial image. A rare reference to such acceptance is to be found in a hand-written journal from Harvard, Massachusetts, dated October 7, 1878, which is now in the collection of the Shaker Community, Hancock, Massachusetts. It says, "Suzie R. went to Ayer to have picture taken."

The reason for the lack of written evidence of the acceptance of images may be surmised and a parallel drawn between it and the total absence of written recordation of woodworking techniques: The Shaker attitude was that woodworking was as natural and vital a function as eating or sleeping or farming, and therefore needed no documentation.

In any case, the Shakers clearly responded as enthusiastically to the new photography as did the world outside. And when they allowed themselves to be photographed, it is evident that they took the trouble to pose carefully so as to present the best possible image to the world.

On January 7, 1839, Louis Daguerre presented a new photographic process to the French Academy of Sciences. The photographs from this process were called daguerreotypes. A silvered copper plate is sensitized by exposure to iodine vapors. The plate is then placed in a camera, and an

---

1. Rules and Orders for the Church of Christ's 2nd Appearing Established by the Ministry & Elders of the Chh. Revised & Reestablished by the Same. New Lebanon, N.Y. May 1860. Copied at South Union, Ky. 1860.

exposure is made. It is removed from the camera and developed by exposing it to mercury vapor, which brings out a single positive image. The use of this process lasted until about 1860. Because of the strict adherence to the Millennial Laws by the Shakers of that time, no daguerreotypes of them are known to exist.

The ambrotype process of photography dates from about 1850. In this process, a light-sensitive wet coating is placed on a sheet of glass, exposed in a camera, and then developed, producing a weak negative image. When it is viewed against a dark background of cloth or paint, a positive image appears. The glass was placed in a hinged leather case to protect it from fading or breaking. The only known example of an ambrotype of a Shaker subject is a photograph of the South Family at Harvard, Massachusetts— perhaps the earliest photograph ever made of a Shaker village (figure 1). Now in the collection of the Museum at Shakertown, South Union, Kentucky, this ambrotype clearly shows the fragility of these images.

The tintype process originated about 1856. In this process, a black-lacquered sheet of iron is coated with a wet emulsion, which is developed after exposure in a camera. As with the daguerreotype and ambrotype, only one image was produced. With the tintype of Elder William Wilson, of Enfield, New Hampshire (figure 3) and with later studio photographs, we begin to see the introduction of the painted studio background. (A later portrait of Elder William appears in the section "Shaker Leaders.") There was a resurgence in popularity of the tintype in the early 1900's. Examples of these are the photographs made of the Shakers from Alfred, Maine, at Old Orchard Beach (figure 4) and at the Boston Picture Tent at Peak's Island, Maine (figure 5).

In 1851, wet collodion glass plates were introduced. Like the ambrotype, these were glass plates coated with a wet emulsion, but now a negative image was achieved and many paper prints could be made from the same negative. It was by this process that Mathew Brady and his men recorded the Civil War. In 1880, the wet-plate era came to an end with the introduction of commercially manufactured dry glass plates, followed by the first flexible transparent photographic film.

The stereoscope, which was invented by an English physicist in 1838, uses two lenses to simulate the vision of human eyes. Two photographs are made simultaneously with one camera through two lenses, and when viewed through the stereoscope, the resultant image is three-dimensional. The first stereograms, stereographs, or stereographic views became popular in the 1850's; these were actually lithographs, sometimes hand-colored. They were replaced by stereo photographs, which reached their greatest popularity in the late 1800's. The Shakers sold sets of stereoscopic views, as well as single

3 Tintype of Elder William Wilson, of Enfield, New Hampshire.

17

4 A tintype of Shakers against a painted studio background.

5 More Shakers pose for their tintype.

6 Brother Nelson Chase, inventor of a folding stereoscope.

stereographic views, to the public in their village stores. They also sold them to other Shaker villages at wholesale prices, for resale in their shops. More than 350 different stereographic views of the Shakers are in existence; an annotated list of them appears at the back of this book, and some of them (single views only) are reproduced in this book.

The importance of the stereographic views in a visual record of Shaker history should not be underestimated. When the popularity of the stereoscope was at its peak, the Shakers, changing with the times, admitted photographers to their villages and permitted them to photograph not only the exteriors of buildings, but the interiors as well. Earlier, "the world's people" had been permitted to enter only the offices and stores of the villages.

Brother Nelson Chase (figure 6) of the community at Enfield, New Hampshire, invented a folding stereoscope and on July 16, 1872, was granted a patent entitled "Chase's Folding Stereoscope Improved." Unfortunately, Brother Nelson's invention, although manufactured, was never marketed. *The Shaker Quarterly* of Spring 1965 quotes a contemporary journal: "After supper we took the stereoscope made by Brother Nelson Chase and made an exhibition of it in several stores. Its neatness, compactness, and general appearance was highly commended by all, but the price was thought to exceed all propriety. The retail price of this one was to be $15.00 . . . per day—with 20 per ct. off at wholesale or by the Doz.—the majority of inspectors thought that Springfield would be a poor market for such an expensive article." [2]

The Shakers traveled widely, for both business and pleasure. Polly Lewis, of the Mount Lebanon community, traveled to Chicago in the late 1880's and while there had portraits made at two different studios on Madison Street—Album Photo, at 335 West Madison, and R. N. Ham, at 387 West Madison (figure 7). Elder Frederick Evans, of the Mount Lebanon community, followed Shaker tenets strictly and in 1871 even took his own Shaker bread to England to eat, but he also sat for his portrait in London and had his name stamped on the face of it (figure 8).

Modern photography was introduced to the Shakers about 1900 by Brother Delmer Wilson of the Sabbathday Lake community in Maine (figure 9). Brother Delmer was an enthusiastic photographer who took hundreds of pictures. Sadly, many of his negatives were destroyed in the fire of the Boys' Shop at Sabbathday Lake on February 21, 1966. The loss of these negatives was tragic, as prints of most of them do not exist.

2. Notes by the way while on a journey to the State of Kentucky in the year 1873. By Henry C. Blinn, Canterbury, N.H. 1873.

7 Portrait of Polly Lewis made in Chicago.

8 Frederick Evans photographed in London.

R. D. Ham, 357 W. MADISON ST., 485 State St, CHICAGO

ELDER FREDERICK W. EVANS,
"SHAKER,"
OF MOUNT LEBANON, NEW YORK, U S.
STEREOSCOPIC CO.   COPYRIGHT.

9 Brother Delmer
Wilson.

10 Brother Delmer's photograph of
Brother Stephen Gowen.

Brother Delmer was not only an avid photographer, but also a resourceful
one. In making an indoor photograph of Brother Stephen Gowen, of Alfred,
Maine, he used an acetylene lamp for illumination (figure 10). Interestingly,
Brother Delmer was also a prolific painter.

We know many Shaker names, but what did they look like? The Shakers
were supposed to be anonymous; they were not supposed to put their names
on clothing or things they made. But they did use their names on the books
and articles they wrote, and they also signed letters. When photography was
accepted, they had many prints made, wrote their names on the backs, and
exchanged them with other communities, just as we do with our families and
friends today, because in the Shaker movement they were all one family
group. Looking through the photographs we begin to connect the face with
the name and what that person did. Once we can associate a name with a
face, we can recognize the face again—older, younger, or with different
wearing apparel. In identifying a Shaker in a photograph, it helps to know
his birth date and the date of his death, the community where he lived, the
trips he took, and the towns around the community where he may have gone
to have photographs taken.

The Shakers were an inventive and progressive people, usually trying out new ideas in advance of their neighbors in "the world." They were among the first people in rural communities to purchase and use new inventions. Their ready acceptance of photography has given us this collection, an invaluable insight into Shaker life that could never be gained from words alone. To quote Laszlo Moholy-Nagy, "The illiterate of the future will be ignorant of pen and camera alike."

ELMER R. PEARSON, associate professor at the Institute of Design of the Illinois Institute of Technology, Chicago, is a trustee of two restored Shaker villages.

11 Ambrotype of Brother Daniel N. Baird of North Union Village, Ohio.

22

JULIA NEAL *The Shakers As They Saw Themselves and As Others Saw Them*

The American Shakers are older than the Republic itself, for the first nine Shakers came from England in 1774. It was not a promising time for British subjects to be coming to the colonies, with hostilities about to erupt any day, but because of the revivalist religious climate soon to hold sway, it did prove to be a favorable moment for the Shakers to arrive.

Leading the little group, then known as The United Believers in the Second Appearing of Christ, was Ann Lee Stanley. With her came her brother William Lee; her niece Nancy Lee; John Hocknell and his son Richard; James Shepherd, a merchant; Mary Partington; James Whittaker; and her husband, Abraham Stanley. Hocknell, a man of property, paid the passage for all of them.

Ann Lee was born in Manchester, England, in 1736, the child of John Lee (or Lees), a blacksmith. The second of eight children, while still a child she helped feed and clothe the family in various ways: by working in a cotton factory, cutting fur for hats, and cooking in a hospital. There was no time for schooling, and so Ann never learned to read and write.

In 1758, at the age of twenty-two, she joined the religious society known as the Shaking Quakers, or Shakers, an offshoot of the French Prophets, or Camisards. The society was in no sense Quaker, except that its leaders, James and Jane Wardley, had been Quakers until they came under the influence of the Camisards, a persecuted Protestant group in France, some of whom had fled to England after the revocation of the Edict of Nantes in 1685.

Ann Lee at first did not play a large part in the group's activities. In 1762 she married Abraham Stanley (or Standerin), who has been described as "a kindly man who loved his beef and beer, his chimney corner and seat in the village tavern." He and Ann had four children, all of whom died in infancy, the last in 1766. Always given to prophetic visions, Ann Lee interpreted these tragedies as a judgment on the sinfulness of sex and marriage. Later she was to affirm: "The marriage of the flesh is a covenant with death and an agreement with hell."

23

The religious meetings of the early Shakers, under the leadership of the Wardleys, resembled the often fanatical and disorderly forms of worship of the Prophets in their home in the Cévennes region of southern France. There were trances, bodily agitations, individual testimonies, and "signs"—heavenly voices and lights. Prophecies and exhortations to repentance were frequent.

The sect attracted new adherents and gradually became more violent in its rejections of "lust" and its denunciation of the Church of England for encouraging the "sinful" marriage state. The Shakers' activities brought down upon them charges of disturbing the peace and eventually provoked acts of oppression and persecution against them. Finally Ann Lee, who had become their leader, was tried for blasphemy, but was acquitted when she convinced the four clergyman judges that she was not a fraud. In 1772, she was imprisoned when she could not pay the fine imposed for disturbing religious services in Christ Church, Manchester. While in jail she experienced a vision that caused her to declare that she was the female incarnation of the word of God. "It is not I that speak," she told the Shakers. "It is Christ who dwells in me."

The classic history of Shakerism first published in 1823, *A Summary View of the Millennial Church of the United Society of Believers*, by Calvin Green and Seth Y. Wells, records that, in another vision, it was revealed to Ann that she was to go to America, where, she was told, the second Christian church would be established.

So it was that on May 19, 1774, the little band of nine Believers set sail from Liverpool on the unseaworthy ship *Mariah* to establish a new faith. Arriving in New York eleven weeks later, the group set about looking for housing and for jobs. Early in 1776 the original Shakers, along with several additional recruits from England, moved to a place seven miles northwest of Albany, to a tract of land that John Hocknell had been able to buy cheaply, and there founded the first Shaker settlement in America, Niskeyuna. No longer with them was Abraham Stanley, who had voyaged to America on the same ship, but who, according to *The Millennial Church*, had "lost all sense and feeling of religion," and had deserted his wife.

Ann Lee directed the group's activities, formulated its doctrines, and conducted religious services, and to her followers had come to be known as Mother Ann, or Ann, the Word. In so addressing her, the Shakers upheld her claim that, just as the male and female are exhibited throughout the animal and vegetable kingdoms, so had God appeared in both forms. The first appearance had been, said *The Millennial Church*, "in the male, in the man Jesus; the second had been in the female—in Ann Lee."

At Niskeyuna, later renamed Watervliet, the first months were spent in

24

clearing the land and erecting log buildings. Much time and labor went into filling the slough holes with brush and with dirt and sand. Morrell Baker, Jr., who wrote the official account, said, "When I consider how much labor we performed and how well we soon began to live under existing circumstances, it seems to me almost a miracle." He added, "In fixing the face of the earth for future generations, we never hired a day's labor to assist us." But war conditions, the scarcity of money, and the Shaker principle of never going into debt soon brought hard times to the new community.

A picture of its destitute condition in 1778 was printed in May 1877 in the society's periodical *The Shaker*:

> Their food consisted principally of rice and milk. A little fish, mostly sturgeon, was everything of the meat kind they enjoyed for several months. Had little or no butter and cheese. . . . They toiled hard for their scanty pittance, and became so reduced in flesh that they looked more like walking skeletons than laboring men.

Relief came when the Shakers were hired by the citizens of Albany to carry donations of food, clothing, and fuel to Crown Point, a famine area. With the money they earned, the brethren purchased needed supplies. Fortunately, too, the crops of 1778 were good.

During the following year, as related by Green and Wells, Mother Ann encouraged her followers by telling them that the time was close at hand when "many would come and embrace the gospel" and directing them to prepare for the enlargement. Her prediction came true. In 1779 a great revival was experienced throughout the area, and religiously-stirred men and women thronged to Watervliet to inquire about the Shaker faith. In 1782, Amos Taylor, a printer of the time and a Shaker apostate, described how there was:

> . . . a constant variety of some newly come and other just ready to leave them;—some would stay two, some six, some ten, and some twenty days on a visit—some would come twice, some thrice, some five, and some ten times a piece; some would come twenty, some fifty, some an hundred, and some two hundred miles.

According to Taylor, the "meetings" generally continued every night until about two o'clock—and very frequently until the break of day.

Another early account was published in 1781 by Valentine Rathbun, of Pittsfield, Massachusetts, a Baptist minister who had embraced the Shaker religion for a time. He recalled from his personal experience how the Shakers approached the inquirer:

25

> . . . and after things are a little settled, they begin . . . telling him that he must confess his sins to them, from his childhood, that they may take his case, and travail for him, that he may be born again. If he be a professor of Godliness, and pleads that he hopes his sins are forgiven, they tell him, nay, they are not forgiven. They tell him whatever is done in secret, must be revealed on the housetop.

The inquirer would then be asked whether he had given his vote and money for the defense of the country and would be instructed that bearing arms was contrary to the gospel.

While some of the Believers talked with the newcomers, others would be singing, wrote Rathbun, "each one his own tune; some without words, in an Indian tune, some jig tunes, some tunes of their own making, in an unknown mutter which they call new tongues."

Having broken his connection with the Believers, Rathbun disapproved of their religious services, saying the activity made "a perfect bedlam" and he could not understand how it could be called the worship of God.

Other apostates, and the general public too, accused the English Shakers of living in drunkenness and debauchery, of having concealed firearms, and of practicing witchcraft. Such reports stimulated investigations by the army and by other religious groups.

In early May 1780, a Baptist committee went to Watervliet from New Lebanon, New York, to investigate "the strange company of English people who had a female leader." The committee's spokesman was Joseph Meacham, originally of Enfield, Connecticut, a Baptist revival leader. After talking to Mother Ann and James Whittaker, Meacham found himself persuaded to the Shaker faith. He soon gave "his wholehearted union to the cause to which he ever after devoted his life." Like Meacham, many who came to investigate remained as converts. On the other hand, many who visited the Shakers went away to redouble the number and vehemence of their derogatory reports.

These attacks only served to increase Shaker zeal. The leaders felt the time had come to embark on missionary tours and to open the gospel publicly. Shaker history does not reveal whether May 19, 1780, was chosen to inaugurate the missionary project because it was the anniversary of the little group's departure from Liverpool, or whether it was chosen as a spontaneous reaction to that strange phenomenon known as "the dark day," taken by many people to be the judgment day.

In his autobiography, Issachar Bates, a Baptist minister and onetime fifer in the Revolutionary War, gave a first-hand account of this day:

> There were neither clouds nor smoke in the atmosphere, yet the sun did not

appear all that day. . . . No work could be done in any houses without a candle! And the night following was as dark accordingly altho' there was a well grown moon! . . . The darkness covered the whole of the land of New England! And what next, right on the back of this came on the Shakers! And that made it darker yet.

Now such confusion of body and mind I had never before witnessed, on the part of the Shakers it was singing, dancing, shouting, shaking, speaking with tongues, turning, preaching, prophesying, and warning the world to confess their sins and turn to God, for His wealth was coming upon them. All this was right in the neighborhood where I lived.

The Shakers' behavior, contrasted with the "cursing, blaspheming . . . and firing pistols" of many other people, convinced Issachar "It was the work of God among the Shakers. But I was not ready yet, for I had married a wife therefore I could not come."

Throughout the remainder of 1780 and during the period between May 1781 and September 1783, Mother Ann and her elders traveled almost constantly in New England to make known their beliefs. The Shaker tenets were so radically different from the prevailing religious and political doctrines of the times that the missionaries met with bitter opposition. Among the Shaker beliefs that aroused hostility were their refusal to take oaths and to bear arms—aggravated by the facts that the Revolution was then in progress and that the Shaker religion and leadership had only recently come from England. Other Shaker doctrines that raised violent fear and suspicion were their celibacy, of course, and additionally, their insistence on perfect obedience and confession to their appointed leaders.

Mobs, instigated by Presbyterian, Baptist, or other denominational ministers and by military authorities, were almost always present to harass the missionaries. In Petersham, Massachusetts, the crowd dragged Mother Ann from her horse, threw her into a sleigh, tore her clothes, and snatched her cap and kerchief, saying they wanted to find out whether she was really a woman. In 1780, Ann, together with the elders, was taken to prison. It was then that some of the public objected to the treatment of the Shakers, pointing out that throwing people in jail on account of their religious convictions was inconsistent with what the colonists themselves were at that very time fighting for—their own civil and religious rights. However, these objections did not deter the enemies of the Shakers. They separated the Shaker leader from her followers and tried to deliver her to the British army. The plan failed, and Ann was again imprisoned, this time in Poughkeepsie. Five months later, some Shaker prisoners in Albany were released, and soon thereafter Mother Ann was also released when Governor Clinton interceded for her.

The missionary group arrived back in Watervliet September 4, 1783,

27

Shaker Societies

LONG-LIVED SOCIETIES			SHORT-LIVED SOCIETIES		
	ESTABLISHED	DISSOLVED	(not indicated on the map)	ESTABLISHED	DISSOLVED
1. Watervliet (Niskeyuna), N.Y.	1787	1938	Gorham, Maine—members moved to New Gloucester, Maine.	1808	1819
2. New (Mount) Lebanon, N.Y.	1787	1947			
3. Hancock, Massachusetts (Shaker Community, Inc., established in 1960 to operate Hancock Shaker Village as a museum open to the public.)	1790	1960	Savoy, Massachusetts— members moved to New Lebanon, Canaan, and Watervliet, New York	1817	1825
4. Enfield, Connecticut	1790	1917	Cheshire, Richmond, and Ashfield, Massachusetts— group meetings in the 1780's were absorbed into the organized communities.	Group Meetings 1780's	
5. Canterbury, New Hampshire	1792	Still Active			
6. Tyringham, Massachusetts	1792	1875			
7. Alfred, Maine	1793	1932			
8. Enfield, New Hampshire	1793	1923	Straight Creek, Ohio	1808	
9. Harvard, Massachusetts	1793	1918	Canaan, New York—Lower Family 1813-1884; Upper Family 1813-1897.	1813	1897
10. Shirley, Massachusetts	1793	1908			
11. Sabbathday Lake (New Gloucester), Maine	1794	Still Active	Darby, Ohio	1822	1823
12. Watervliet (Beulah), Ohio	1806	1910	Sodus Bay, Sodus Point, or Port Bay, New York— members moved to Grove- land, N.Y.	1826	1836
13. Pleasant Hill, Kentucky (Independent, non-profit, corporation organized in 1961 to operate Pleasant Hill; opened to the public as a museum in 1968.)	1806	1910	Philadelphia, Pennsylvania— moved to Watervliet after a few years. Revived tem- porarily in 1860.	1846	
14. South Union, Kentucky	1807-10	1922	Narcoossee, Florida—branch of New Lebanon, New York, existed several years.	1894	
15. West Union (Busro), Indiana	1810-11	1827			
16. North Union (Cleveland), Ohio	1822	1889	White Oak, Georgia—soon abandoned.	1898	
17. Whitewater, Ohio	1824-25	1907			
18. Groveland, New York	1836	1895			

literally worn out, having been absent two years and three months. They had laid the foundations for a number of new Shaker communities that were to be consolidated later. Although Ann Lee had achieved much, hardship and persecution had been her lot almost from the day she had joined the Shakers twenty-two years before. In the following year, 1784, the young society was to lose two of its original leaders through the deaths of Elder William Lee on July 21, and of Mother Ann on September 8. Ann was forty-eight, her brother, forty-four.

It was felt by her enemies that with Mother Ann dead "the delusion would soon be at an end." Perhaps some of the followers, too, felt that their little world might collapse. But James Whittaker, Mother Ann's successor, began a strong program to weld the separated groups into a more united body. Father James revisited every place the gospel had been received, teaching and encouraging the young converts. In addition he extended the work into Maine. While he was staying with the Believers in Enfield, Connecticut, he died, on July 20, 1787, at the age of thirty-six.

The leadership now fell for the first time to an American convert—Joseph Mcacham, of New Lebanon, the former Baptist revival leader. Father Joseph has been described as being a noble and attractive man, "tall, erect, somewhat slender, with broad shoulders and full chest, dignified and graceful in his bearing." But he was "entirely lacking in natural ability for the movements and exercises employed in worship." He made up for this deficiency by practicing the exercises so energetically in a vacant room over a shop that the floorboards were worn smooth. Many of his "laboring" exercises Father Joseph claimed were revealed to him in visions, and he in turn taught them to Mother's children.

One of Father Joseph's first acts was to name Lucy Wright to be the female head of the ministry. Lucy, a native of Pittsfield, and her husband, Elizur Goodrich, had early been converted to Shakerism. Mother Ann valued Lucy highly and depended on her greatly during the time of her missionary journeys and her imprisonment. Father Joseph's appointment of Lucy was a natural continuation of the tradition of dual leadership implicit in Mother Ann's claim to be the female counterpart of Jesus Christ, a tradition that had begun with Jane Wardley and continued with Ann Lee.

Father Joseph and Mother Lucy went to work to carry forward a plan to bring all the scattered Believers to New Lebanon, New York, and establish a formal society. Word was sent out in September 1787, and by December of that year the Believers began to gather. Industries were begun, buildings erected, and each person labored daily at his particular craft or skill, for the common good. The communal Christmas dinner held at New Lebanon in

1787 marked the actual beginning of the New Lebanon society and of Shakerism as a religious institution.

Although the earlier leaders had not been clearly aware of it, by the time of this gathering, Father Joseph knew that the Shakers must live apart from the world in their own communities, with all resources held in common. He realized that the only economic system that would be consistent with their basic beliefs would have to be autonomous, communistic, and self-sufficient. The Shakers were not laboring for profit, their aim was to live perfect lives, and so the goods they produced were extremely well made, their agricultural produce of the highest quality. They abhorred extravagance and excess, and so their products exhibited an elegant simplicity. Because of these attributes, and the honest dealings of the Shakers, their wares would always find ready markets, and the societies never had trouble in being self-supporting so long as the craft system remained the basis of the country's economy.

The "family" form of organization of Shaker communities began to take shape about this time, the outgrowth of Father Joseph's preliminary organization into classes, or orders, in 1788. When the system had been fully worked out, government of each family was placed in the hands of elders and eldresses, two of each sex in each family. Business transactions and dealings with "the world" were entrusted to deacons and deaconesses, or trustees. The highest offices of any Shaker society were those of the ministry—one man and one woman for each society of Believers—and over all the ministries formed then or in the future the one at New Lebanon would have authority and jurisdiction.

In 1792, New Lebanon was fully established "in Gospel Order," and the lead, or ministry, was quite naturally headed by Father Joseph Meacham and Mother Lucy Wright. Since it was the first fully established community, New Lebanon, later called Mount Lebanon, was considered "the Centre of Union" for all Shakers.

Before his death in 1796, Father Joseph saw formal organization effected for ten other societies: Watervliet in 1787; Hancock, Massachusetts, 1790; Enfield, Connecticut, 1791–92; Canterbury, New Hampshire, and Tyringham, Massachusetts, 1792; Enfield, New Hampshire, Alfred, Maine, and Harvard and Shirley, Massachusetts, 1793; and New Gloucester (later Sabbathday Lake), Maine, 1794.

It is remarkable that only twenty years after arriving in the colonies and only fourteen years after opening their testimony publicly, the Shakers had succeeded in establishing eleven societies in five states. These eleven societies, with their hierarchies of elders and eldresses, deacons and trustees, then entered a busy period of erecting needed buildings, clearing and farming their land, and establishing numerous industries.

30

Because they had limited tools with which to cut and dress their lumber and their stone, the practical brethren at first constructed small houses with narrow halls and steep stairs in order to conserve materials. Many of these first buildings went unpainted. Later, when larger buildings could be constructed, none received more attention than the meeting houses and the barns, for it was these buildings that symbolized the cardinal Shaker principles of worship and work. For example, the second meeting house at New Lebanon was ready for use in 1824. It had an arched, or "boiler," roof—of slate supported by bent timbers. It was built by Moses Johnson, who planned and built most of the eastern Shaker meeting houses.

Bernard Karl, Duke of Saxe-Weimar-Eisenach, visited New Lebanon in 1825. In his book *Travels Through North America 1825–26*, he described the white frame meeting house as being eighty feet long and about fifty broad:

> On one side stand benches in form of an amphitheatre for spectators and old members to whom dancing has become difficult. The floor consists of handsome cedar wood, which is well polished; the boards are attached to each other without nails.

The English editor Hepworth Dixon, in his *New America*, described the same

12 Mount Lebanon, New York. South Family Shakers returning from church. The four-story dwelling house is at the center, the second meeting house is second from right, and the first meeting house is at the far right. Originally, the first meeting house had a gambrel roof, which was lifted in order to add two floors to convert the structure into an herb house with a flat roof.

building as "a spacious, airy edifice" and "plain as a plank."

Charles Daubenny, an English scientist, visited the meeting house and noticed especially the "large wooden sounding board, extending about half way from the centre of the room to either end, as a means of assisting their voices in singing."

The large New Lebanon barn with entrances on five levels also caught the attention of visitors. Dixon spoke of it as "an edifice of stone in a region of sheds and booths . . . a very fine barn, the largest (I am told) in America," combining cowshed, hayloft, and storehouse "of singular size and happy contrivance." He observed, "The Granary is to a Shaker what the temple was to the Jew."

Visitors to the Hancock society have always found unusual and exciting the large round stone barn which housed fifty-two head of cattle and two span of horses. J. E. A. Smith (Godfrey Greylock), a respected historian, in a book published in 1852, *Taghconic, or Letters and Legends*, said he considered the Hancock barn "the best model . . . to be found for a building of the kind; it is certainly the noblest looking agricultural structure I ever saw."

Although they were busy with their building and development program, the faithful followers of Mother Ann did not forget their missionary work. Soon they began to think of new frontiers. Mother Ann herself prophesied before her death that there would come a great religious revival in the Southwest and directed that at that time the Shaker gospel should be opened. As she foretold, the revival occurred. During the years between 1801 and 1804, the eastern newspapers carried accounts of a great revival in Kentucky and the neighboring states of Ohio and Tennessee. The Shaker leaders recalled that the eastern societies had been born in a time of revivalism, so they began to feel "the gift" to send missionaries westward to the seat of the new revival.

The task fell to Benjamin Seth Youngs, John Meacham, son of Joseph, and Issachar Bates, who had first met the Shakers on the famous dark day and had later brought his wife and seven of his children into the faith. An account of that first westward journey and of the subsequent implantation of the Shaker religion is given by Bates in the *Sketch*, a memoir he wrote later of his own life and experiences.

The men carried a letter of counsel, admonishing them "not to look or listen after the affairs of the world . . . not to be looking after the curiosities or new things that are pleasing to nature . . . and not to dispute the gospel with any insincere person, for such argument would be of no avail." They carried a second letter, a pastoral letter to the future western converts. Also entrusted to their care was the sum of $5,467, to be used in sustaining themselves and their endeavors until they could become independent.

Since the winter weather made the back roads impassable, the men traveled the main stage road to Philadelphia, Baltimore, and Washington. Continuing through Virginia, they arrived in Tennessee, where they went through Bean Station and thence over the Clinch Mountains into Kentucky.

When they arrived there on March 1, the men at once began to hear much about the great revival. They had no difficulty in becoming acquainted with some of the revival preachers—Barton Stone, John Thompson, Matthew Houston, and others. Finding that the revival fires which had started in the Kentucky counties of Logan and Christian were now burning brightest across the Ohio River, the men pushed on to Warren County, Ohio, where on March 22 they arrived at the double log house of Malcolm Worley. They could rest at last after two months and twenty-two days of a 1,233-mile journey.

For that time, Worley was a well-educated and well-to-do man. Because of his education and wealth, he was a prominent citizen in his community and a leading member of the Turtle Creek Presbyterian Congregation, which had recently rejected Calvinist doctrines and had become known as "New Lights." Worley and his wife talked to the three Shakers for most of the night to learn about them and what had motivated them to make such a long and arduous trip.

Excited by the new testimony, Worley was anxious to have his own minister, Richard McNemar, meet the missionaries from New York State. McNemar spent an entire day with the visitors and later wrote, "I judged them to be men of honest principles, singular piety, and of a deep understanding in the things of God, and as such I determined to treat them so long as their deportment was correspondent."

The next day, Sunday, the Shakers attended services, where McNemar preached much to their satisfaction. Asked to speak, Issachar "spoke short," followed by Benjamin, who read the New Lebanon pastoral letter.

But the reception on that first Sunday was in sharp contrast to their reception later throughout the territory. When they began to win converts—notably Malcolm Worley, Richard McNemar, and most of the Turtle Creek Congregation—they found themselves again objects of suspicion and persecution. The missionaries soon realized they were to meet with as much mob violence in the West as the first Shakers had in the East.

In 1805, two months after their arrival in Ohio, the first society in the West, Union Village, was established near Lebanon, Ohio. But, as Issachar Bates relates in his *Sketch*, the alarmed church leaders of the area denounced the Shakers as "Seducers, Deceivers, Liars, Wolves in sheep's clothing—parting man and wife and breaking up families and churches."

Bates describes how it was soon whispered among the New Lights that the Shakers castrated all their males and that they "stripped and danced naked in their night meetings and then went into a promiscuous debauch." Babies born of the unlawful embraces were said to be concealed by murdering them. Issachar, of course, regarded the rumors as "the croaking of bullfrogs" and was glad to find that the new Believers stood the storm firmly. Such opposition merely stirred the three New Yorkers to go "through the wild wooden world by day and night hunting up every soul that God had been preparing for eternal life."

In June, additional easterners were sent out to help in the work. When Elder David Darrow, Daniel Moseley, and Solomon King arrived to take over supervision of Union Village, the veterans went on to spread the faith through Ohio and Kentucky.

In the fall of 1805, a man named Sewell, who did not want to live near the Shakers, offered to sell them a quarter section of land—that is, a tract half a mile square, containing 160 acres. Issachar was chosen to go back to New Lebanon to secure the price of $1,640. On September 26, he started on foot along the Chillicothe road, described in 1806 by Thomas Ashe in his *Travels in America* as being "no more than a path through a wood, the trees marked with an axe to indicate the direction," and leading "for the most part through a forest swamp."

Back in New Lebanon after a difficult journey, Issachar gave a full account of the first six months of frontier mission work. Then with the money that was quickly raised and with "as much love and power as he could hold" he returned alone 776 miles to Union Village. Learning that there had been many more converts during his absence, he wrote, "The devil was mad about it and I was glad about it."

Encouraged by the financial support and the expression of love brought from the East, Elder David bought Sewell's land for Union Village. His people began clearing and planting it and then undertook an extensive building program.

The next May the New Lebanon ministry sent out nine more reinforcements. Among these were three women—Ruth Darrow, daughter of the Union Village elder, Molly Goodrich, and Ruth Farrington, who was to serve as first eldress in the ministry with Elder David.

Molly Goodrich wrote to the New Lebanon sisters in August 1806, describing the hardships of the "long and tedious and very wearisome journey." From Molly's letter it becomes clear that being a Shaker missionary required great dedication and stamina. She wrote of how seven days were needed to climb on foot the various ranges of the Alleghenies, how they could not see the ground for the rocks and stones, and how going

34

over the mountains the chests in the wagons "pitch forward and split the bottoms very much." But even the roughness of the mountains was exceeded by the roughness of the Ohio roads. Molly wrote:

> After we got into the state of Ohio we encountered extremely deep mud holes and mire holes and swamps so bad we can not communicate it to you . . . first down the horses would go up to their bellies. Then they would rise and again the fore wheels of the waggon would go down to such a degree that the hind end of the waggon would seem to set up nearly straight and at other times the waggon would lie on one side and again on the other side.

Food was scarce and there was seldom anything fresh. There were eleven ferries to cross and ten creeks to be forded, with the water usually covering the hubs of the wheels. It rained fourteen of the forty-one days. Many nights had to be spent drying out their clothes and their provisions. In the sixth week they arrived at Chillicothe, where "about a mile out of town just before sunset" they were met by the brethren. In Molly's understated words, "It was a very happy meeting."

The next day, the Union Villagers took some of the "loading into their wagons" and the men "went on before us with their axes, cutting out new roads and making bridges, for it was a continual swamp for three days after they met us." As they approached Union Village, the road was better. (Thomas Ashe's account of that year reported that the land "nearest the Shaker village was chequered with improvements.") Arriving at Malcolm Worley's cabin, they were received kindly by all the brethren and Malcolm and his wife made them "welcome home."

The next day being Sunday, they attended meeting, and on Monday they "walked out to see our little cabin which is the house we are to move into." The cabin was eighteen by twenty feet with one room below and a loft chamber above. The loft chamber floor was "loose boards laid down . . . with large cracks . . . much more open than the Eastern barns." But true to their practical inventiveness, the newcomers "stopped the cracks with sticks of wood corking them with tow."

The Eastern sisters found the Ohio brethren very much in need of their help. Their clothes were in disrepair and some of the men were ill because "the western manner of cooking and diet" was so different from that in the East. Elder David was especially weak. The loving care the sisters gave him must have restored his health, for he was to serve as elder another nineteen years.

Molly's letter was not one of complaint, for she wrote, "We have learned in whatever state our lot is cast therewith to be content," but she wrote also, "We used to think we knew what hardship was, and truly we did, but we

35

knew nothing about it to what we know now."

The sisters back at New Lebanon must have rejoiced that Molly had found "a people that loved the gospel" and had "the gifts and power of God among them in shaking, turning, leaping, clapping hands, shouting, and some have the gift of tongues."

In his history of Union Village, J. P. MacLean tells how the enthusiastic new Ohio converts at first held their religious services in Richard McNemar's double log cabin, using the dog-trot for their shaking and marching exercises. Later, an outdoor wooden platform resembling a threshing floor was constructed and used for the services until the first meeting house was completed in 1809. All the early buildings were constructed with simple tools and mechanical aids created with the help of Joseph Allen, a good mechanic who had come from the Tyringham, Massachusetts, society.

From 1812, when the Warren County Shakers signed their first covenant and became a fully organized society, Union Village became the Mother, or governing, society in the West. Under the evangelistic efforts of the veteran missionaries, aided by their strongest converts, four other colonies were gathered. These were Beulah (or Watervliet), Ohio, 1806; Shawnee Run (or Pleasant Hill), Mercer County, Kentucky, also 1806; Gasper (or South Union), Logan County, Kentucky, 1807; and Busro (or West Union), Indiana, 1810. A little later came North Union, Warrensville Township, Ohio, gathered in 1812 and organized in 1826; and Whitewater in Hamilton and Butler counties, Ohio, gathered and organized in 1824.

The pattern by which the western societies were established was very similar to the way those in the East were established. Lands and houses of the first converts determined the location of the colony. Society affairs were first under the direction of one of the original leaders and then responsibility was placed in the hands of a strong early convert.

The new western societies threw their full efforts into clearing and sowing their land, planting orchards, constructing essential buildings, establishing industries, and opening up avenues of trade, all the while striving to enlarge their membership. Nevertheless, the early years brought some pinching times. Whitewater had such a hard first winter it was recorded in the society records that "it was Lent with them nearly all the year round." Hervey Eades recalled the years between 1810 and 1815 at South Union, when as a young child he had only half as much mush and milk as he craved. But hard work, determined effort, and strong leadership overcame reverses and hardships. Attractive villages emerged. Cultivated fields, well-tended gardens, and productive orchards became the hallmark of the western societies.

The Shakers' economic progress, coupled with their spiritual growth, fanned feelings of distrust and jealousy. Not only rival religious groups, but relatives and friends of members who had given their property to the society found the Shakers suspect. There were soon threats against them. In his *Sketch*, Bates tells of how he, Malcolm Worley, and Matthew Houston were traveling near Vincennes, Indiana, when twelve men on horseback came up with ropes to bind them. Eventually the Shakers were released, but since muster day was imminent in Vincennes, the brethren expected further trouble, so they appealed to William Henry Harrison, governor of the Territory of Indiana, who sent a magistrate and a constable for their protection. The Shakers had earlier been assured by Harrison that the laws of the territory would protect them, that they had a right to preach the faith, and anyone had a right to embrace it.

There were many instances of mobs attacking the Shakers. On August 27, 1810, for example, five hundred armed men, joined by nearly two thousand onlookers, marched on Union Village. Benjamin Seth Youngs, who witnessed the scene, thought that the presence and efforts of Francis Dunlavy, first circuit judge of Ohio, and of the uniformed troops, prevented the eruption of real violence. Dunlavy proposed a plan whereby representatives from the mob and from the Shakers would meet to discuss their differences. It was agreed that a committee from the objectors should enter the dwelling houses to question the sisters about life within the society. The committee was also to inspect the school. After their tour of inspection, the committee reported that they did not find "the enslaved woman" who had been reported, but instead found "a decent house with decent people in it." They had seen "Testaments in abundance" in the school, therefore it could not be true that Shaker children were not allowed to read the Bible. Finally the protesters dispersed.

But this was not to be the last mob. Although objectors usually claimed recovery of children or property as their motivation, other factors also evoked bitter opposition. At Busro, Indiana, it was the Shakers' pacifist principles. It was just the period when tension was highest between the Indians and the settlers, and the fact that the non-violent Shakers would not join the settlers against the Indians brought charges that the Shakers and the Indians were conspiring to take the settlers' lands. Animosity intensified when it became known that some Indians had had their farming tools repaired by the Busro Shakers.

Feelings were calmed somewhat when Governor Harrison directed the Shakers to feed the Indians and treat them kindly but not to do their smith work any more. Later, some Indians stole seven of the Shakers' best horses. This incident was said to have "opened the eyes of their neighbors, as it showed that the Believers had no secret understanding with the Indians."

With the onset of the War of 1812, the society met new hardships. Three military companies quartered at Busro took over the elders' shop as a commissary and made the dooryard into a slaughteryard. Issachar Bates said the Indiana Shakers felt "the kind hand of God was stretched out a little" to help them, when Colonel Boyd of Boston arrived and "bore testimony in Vincennes and elsewhere that 'the Shakers at the East were the best people on earth.'" The Colonel appeared to be "glad to see us as though we were his natural kin," and his attitude helped "blunt the edge off every weapon formed against us."

Another ally was a Kentuckian, Colonel Daves, who was acquainted with the Believers at Pleasant Hill. He advised the brethren to call upon the governor for relief from the fines that were accumulating as a result of their non-compliance with military conscription. Help did come from Governor Harrison later, after he was elected a member of the Ohio legislature. Then Harrison's influence helped bring about the passage of a regulation which allowed the Shaker men to perform three days of road work instead of the required three days of military drill.

The War of 1812 brought distress to other Shaker colonies besides Busro. At South Union, Kentucky, for example, the brothers each had to pay a one-hundred-dollar fine when they would not submit to the draft. Also, the village was often disturbed by soldiers camping at their spring or searching for Indians who had been reported to be at the Shakers' Sunday services.

In addition to mob action and the persecution of individuals that they suffered, the Shakers in both eastern and western societies were often victims of incendiaries. They were also frequently involved in legal actions by persons seeking to recover property which had been given the society. Although most of the court cases were decided in favor of the Shakers, these lawsuits were extremely costly in time and money. It is ironic that the Shakers, who governed themselves entirely, neither voting nor wishing to cause trouble in any way, and paying their taxes faithfully, should so often have been involved in troublesome litigation.

From 1830 to 1860, the American Shakers enjoyed their most successful period of community living and met increased social acceptance. Animosity was gradually replaced by both natural curiosity and genuine interest on the part of "the world's people."

The nineteenth century brought improved transportation, which encouraged travel not only by Americans but also by people from abroad. The Utopian Shaker villages were favorite stopping-places for travelers, and many of these travelers published their impressions in travel books or in the periodicals of the time. The consensus was that the Shaker communities were neat and orderly, prosperous, and quiet.

Fredericka Bremer, a Swedish novelist, who visited New Lebanon about

13 Fred Faulbaker-Sturr, an elder at Whitewater, Ohio, in front of the meeting house.

1853, thought that the village, with its pale yellow, two-storied wooden houses, built in good proportion and standing on green slopes, produced "a very lovely and romantically idyllian scene." She wrote that, "Life at New Lebanon did not look to me so gloomy or so contracted as I had imagined." Visiting later at Canterbury, New Hampshire, Bremer reported the village "as quiet and as orderly as if a life of labor did not exist there. . . . [It] almost struck the mind as something spiritual."

A hiker in the Berkshires found the New Lebanon stables "cleaner than most of the New York tenement houses," and "the stone walls . . . the best laid and most solid that can be seen in the country."

A correspondent of the English *Penny Magazine* wrote, "The road through the settlement had not a stone bigger than a walnut upon it." "The windows were so clear," he said, "they seemed to have no glass in them," and the floors were "as even and almost as white as marble." Outside the houses, "The wood was put up in piles, supported by stone corner posts—and not a chip was astray, not a log awry."

In 1867, when Hepworth Dixon visited New Lebanon, he thought the walls appeared "as if they had been built yesterday." He added that the windows had large glass panes and that the curtains and blinds were "spotless white." Furthermore, the cleanliness extended beyond the houses to the "clean roads and trim hedges." Dixon concluded that:

> . . . the men who till these fields, tend these gardens, who bind these sheaves, who turn these vines, who plant these apple trees have been drawn into putting their love into the daily life.

39

The western villages also had many visitors. One described the Union Village acres as "slightly rolling land, any part of which would make glad the heart of a Pennsylvania hillside farmer."

In his *Journals in the United States and Lower Canada*, published in 1817, John Palmer voiced surprise at finding "eccentric people" possessed of the best farms he had seen in America during his visit. He was also surprised to find their cows and horses looked "remarkably well."

On his first visit to Whitewater, J. P. MacLean, the Ohio geologist and Shaker historian, said he knew he was on the society lands the moment he struck them, for "the fences were in good condition, the lands cared for, and there was the general aspect of thriftiness." His opinion was confirmed as soon as he caught sight of buildings of "solid appearance and want of decoration."

There were, however, travelers who took a different view of the quietness and the orderliness of the Shaker premises. Parker Willis, American editor, thought Pleasant Hill looked "too virtuous for comfort." He wrote in 1854, "I never saw such excessive neatness. The stones of the walls look as exemplary as if every one had been catechised and wiped clean with the corner of an apron." Willis was probably speaking of the limestone walls of the large 1825 Centre House and of several other smaller buildings. As a New Englander, he undoubtedly looked closely at the twenty miles of stone walls that enclosed the Shakers' Kentucky fields.

Amelia Murray, Lady of the Bedchamber to Queen Victoria, reported that at least one Shaker woman revolted against the quietness of her village when she "left and engaged herself in one of the most noisy factories she could find." Amelia, a Londoner, supposed "the contrast was agreeable."

Many visitors were unaware that Shakers were free to leave the society at any time. Dixon, for example, thought it important to report, "Those who have come into union came unsought; those who would go may retire unheeded." Hervey Eades, a South Union elder, claimed that "a Shaker is the freest soul on earth because all his bonds are self-imposed." Eades could have told Dixon that, although a novitiate or a covenant member was free to leave, a departure did not go "unheeded." The ministry usually regretted the "turning-back," but in the case of an obvious weakling or trouble-maker they felt relief.

Most visitors found the Shaker women unattractive—"pale and wan," "pale and sallow," or "pale and devoid of color"—so that sitting as they did with their arms crossed before them they looked like so many statues. An English naval officer, Captain Marryat, stated explicitly that the women were "so unearthly in their complexions that they looked as if they had been taken up from their coffins a few hours after their decease. . . . One

40

cadaverous yellow tinge prevailed."

Visiting at Union Village in the early 1820's, the Duke of Saxe-Weimar saw among the Ohio women "some very pretty faces, but they were all without exception of a pale and sickly hue." He added that he saw eight or ten women going about who "turned in their toes and elbows as if carefully taught to be ungraceful."

The nineteenth-century costumes worn by the Shaker sisters were not generally admired. Marianne Finch, in *An Englishwoman's Experience in America*, thought the dress worn in the 1850's by the Shaker women was:

> certainly the most ingenious device that was ever contrived for concealing all personal advantages. A bulbous, one-shaped muslin cap, that holds all the hair and covers half the face; a long narrow dress with the waist at the arm-pits, so fashioned that the shoulders all look equally high; the neck covered with a little square white handkerchief, pinned down before, and a pocket handkerchief folded in a small square, and pinned near the region of the heart or thrown waiterwise over the arm, constitute a costume that would disfigure the very Goddess of Beauty.

Fredericka Bremer observed that the caps were "very much blued, which still more increased the deathlike hue of the countenance." The entire costume "seemed intended to make the whole body look like a tree-stem, without any curved lines."

The dress and general appearance of the Shaker brothers was also frequently described in the travel accounts. Charles Daubenny wrote:

> the males were dressed . . . in dark trowsers, and other habiliments corresponding to those a respectable laborer in this country or a farmer in England would wear. They were in general a harsh forbidding set of men, with a peculiar solemn, gloomy, ascetic, and rather stolid expression of countenance. . . . Their hair was allowed to grow behind and was combed straight, so that it hung over their back and shoulders.

Another writer thought that the "odd manner in which the hair is cut" gave the men a "very singular appearance"; but he thought the men generally looked "healthy and ruddy."

Patterns for the Shaker clothes changed with some regularity. The author of *Letters on Kentucky* reported that in 1825 the men at Pleasant Hill were wearing suits of light-colored domestic cloth, with coats and waistcoats of the long worsted fashion, "with outer pockets in the former, half way down the leg, and those in the waistcoats resting on the hips. Their shirts were of coarse cotton and they were without neck-cloths." In 1853, the New York Shaker brothers were wearing "knee-breeches, stockings, and high-heeled shoes" to Sunday services. (The high heel worn at times by both the Shaker men and Shaker women was comparable to the modern stacked heel.)

In 1825, Pleasant Hill women wore long-waisted gowns of dark color, long checked aprons extending to the neck, and white long-eared caps. The usual white kerchief was thrown over the shoulders, but the handkerchief hanging over the arm was of a checked cloth.

Almost every nineteenth-century visitor to a Shaker colony managed to attend a public service on Sunday. The written accounts deal mostly with the "exercising or marching," giving the position of the singers and dancers, describing the movements, especially the use of the hands and feet, and commenting on the music.

A typical account is that of Charles Daubenny, who visited New Lebanon in the early 1840's:

> The ceremony began by the removal of the benches and the marshalling of the men and women in two separate battalions oppositely placed one to the other. . . . The lines extended nearly to the middle of the room, leaving, however, a small interval between the men and women, in order to give space for one of the elders to get up and address the persons present, and in order that he might be heard and seen by strangers beyond . . . the ranks on both sides slightly receded more and more as they approached the side in which the latter were stationed. Being thus marshalled, they began their religious exercises by a song or chaunt, very monotonous and somewhat harsh and grating accompanied by a gentle stamping of the feet, which seemed intended to keep time with their voices.
>
> . . . The first dance consisted in a slow advance, of all the men and women, five or six paces toward the wall, who then wheeled round and proceeded the same number of steps in the direction in which the spectators were placed. All this was done with the utmost gravity, and the most unbinding rigidity of feature; the feet performing a sort of measured step, but the other parts of the body stiffened as though they were parts of so many automata.

When the dance was completed, the elder addressed the spectators, requesting them "not to interrupt the proceedings" by getting up on the benches or talking to their neighbors.

Another dance was performed during which the participants became greatly agitated, whisking "round and round with the greatest rapidity." Indeed, "Several of the women appeared to be thrown into violent hystericks." And one girl, "threw up her handkerchief into the air, tore off her cap, and required the care of two or three older women to hold her down." One man, "rather stout and short with a large bald head . . . shook his head, squatted nearly down on the ground, rose again, whisked round and round, and performed various other fantastic evolutions."

Visitors expressed various reactions to the Shaker dance. James Stuart, an

Edinburgh man visiting in the late 1820's, simply echoed the Shaker view that "the hands and feet, which are useful to man in his own service, ought also to be employed in the worship of God." Bremer did not see why "dancing might not constitute worship as well as singing and other modes of action," but she found that the Shaker congregation lacked the exaltation felt by King David when he danced for joy before the ark. Horace Greeley wrote: "We hear of people crucifying their sinful afflictions, everywhere; it is here alone that we are permitted to observe the process."

Captain Marryat found the dancing "very absurd" and said he would have laughed had he not "felt disgusted at such a degradation of rational and immortal beings."

Visitors who remained in the villages overnight or for several days found much of interest. At Hancock, Massachusetts, one visitor, Charles M. Skinner, thought the cooking "worthy of Delmonico's" and considered his lunch of sixteen items for 25¢ a great bargain.

A correspondent of *The Penny Magazine* in 1837 described a special lunch as being made up of delicious bread—some wheaten, some of Indian corn, and some made with molasses; cheese, butter, spring water, and excellent currant wine." He thought the visiting group "could have gone on eating such bread and butter all day."

The guest rooms were described as being large and light, with everything neat and convenient, but containing nothing decorative. One visitor found his room "painfully bright and clean."

Hervey Elkins, of Enfield, New Hampshire, explained the furnishings in terms of the Millennial Laws:

> Plain chairs, bottomed with rattan or rush, and light so as to be easily portable; one rocking chair is admissible in each room, but such a luxury is unencouraged; one or two writing tables or desks; one looking glass, not exceeding eighteen inches in length, set in a plain mahogany frame; an elegant but plain stove; two lamps; one candle stand . . . bedsteads painted green; coverlets of a mixed color, blue and white; carpets manufactured by themselves, and each containing but three colors; two or three Bibles and all the religious works by the Society, a concordance, grammar, dictionary, etc. . . . . No image or portrait of anything upon the earth, or under the earth . . . consequently clocks and such articles, purchased of the world, go through the process of having all their superficial decorations erased from their surfaces.

In 1837 Harriet Martineau, the English author, complimented the Shakers' housekeeping, as evidenced in "their stair carpets, the feet of their chairs, the springs of their grates, and their spitting boxes—for even these neat people have spitting boxes." She thought the Shakers showed a "nicety which is rare in America." Marianne Finch wrote, "The meeting house is not open to strangers if it rains, on account of the dirt they introduce, and I do not wonder at it, for I never saw any place so exquisitely clean."

One visitor expressed amazement on learning that a New Lebanon dwelling house had 170 drawers in the attic for storing clothes and that another house had 360 drawers, about 9 to every inhabitant. Mother Ann's children were always taught to keep everything in its place so it could be found by night as well as by day. The more observant of the visitors became aware that the multiple drawers were an extension of the Shaker principle of functionalism.

The question of whether or not equality existed among the communal Shakers was of considerable interest to visitors. W. N. Blaney, an English gentleman who visited the United States in 1822–23, thought that, "Like all sects that pretend to the community of goods, the rule of equality is not strictly adhered to." According to him, "The Elders, and chief men or women, are much better off than the rest, live in better houses, and have better fare." Other commentators supported Blaney's accusation, but all agreed that "no one may be an idler not even under the pretense of study, thought and contemplation."

Dixon reported, "Every man among the brethren has a trade; some of them have two, even three or four trades . . . everyone must follow his occupation, however high his rank and calling in the church." As for the sisters, Dixon learned that all were employed:

> . . . some in the kitchen, some in waiting on others (duties which they take in turn, a month for each course), some in weaving cloth, some in preserving fruit, some in distilling essences, some in making fans and knick-knacks. Maple syrup is an article for which they have a good demand; they make rose water, cherry water, peach water; they sew, they sing, they teach children, and teach them well.

When Marianne Finch asked an elder about equality between men and women, she was told:

> Yes . . . we associate with women in everything; in our government, in our religion, in our social affairs, she stands beside us—not as our property, but as our equal and helpmate. We have the same moral code; and the same obedience to it is required from both sexes.

In addition to having a single standard and voting rights, the Shaker sister had the privilege of confessing her faults to another sister rather than to a brother.

The racial equality that existed among the Shakers was noted and reported as being exceptional at the time. In his 1825 *Letters on Kentucky*, an

44

anonymous visitor to Pleasant Hill wrote, "The blacks of each sex were arranged indiscriminately in the same ranks, and attired in the same manner as the whites."

An anonymous visitor in the East listed as one of her "peculiarities of the Shakers" that in an 1832 church service there were "several coloured persons, male and female, who are dressed in the same costume as the other members and joined with them in the dance."

Published accounts of Shaker life from 1820 to 1870 contain many personal observations from which emerges the Shaker image of that period. One learns that the Shakers were unusually healthy, that they were almost fanatic about ventilation, that longevity became characteristic of the sect, and that the aged received very good care, each having a "ministering angel" assigned to him or her. One learns also that laughter came easily, that humility was much stressed, and that "union meetings" were held in which small groups of men and women conversed simply and said "agreeable things about nothing . . . as common there as elsewhere."

It is clear from their accounts that most who went to visit the Shaker communities did so after having heard "many strange stories about the worship and doctrines of this remarkable people."

After his visit in 1822, Blaney kept his preconceived opinion, for he wrote:

> I cannot but think that it is rather a disgrace to the 19th century for a sect to exist and flourish which not only praises the Great Spirit by dancing but even believes that Ann Lee, the drunken profligate wife of an English blacksmith, is co-equal and co-eternal with the Deity.

In 1825, a gentleman, probably a Virginian, wrote a friend that the Kentucky Shakers blended much "theological absurdity with practical sobriety and common sense," and it was his opinion that they had suffered from many "unjust slanders."

In 1828, the Duke of Saxe-Weimar could not endorse the Shaker tenet of celibacy, but he did remark facetiously, "In countries . . . with too great population, it might perhaps be of service . . . if the Shaker missionaries could make some proselyting trips there."

Harriet Martineau concluded, "Whatever they have peculiarly good among them is owing to the soundness of their economical principles."

Bremer and Finch agreed that the Shaker communities filled a real need as havens for the "shipwrecked in life . . . the solitary and the feeble . . . the children of misfortunes." Finch felt the orphan would be given "a good plain education and some useful occupation by which to earn a living." She admitted that some of her former negative opinions had been erased by more intimate acquaintance and that the Shakers' success was "a sufficient

45

refutation of their being hypocrites and ignorant fanatics." She further stated:

> If the Shaker society had not been true to its convictions and its objects, it could not have established itself, much less made itself trusted and respected in the heart of this great republic so opposed to it in all its ends and aims. The ruling principles of one being obedience and self-denial; those of the other liberty and expansion.

The Scot James Stuart in 1833 measured the Shakers against the followers of Robert Owen, the Welsh socialist who founded a cooperative community in New Harmony, Indiana. He concluded that although the Shaker mode of living required greater self-denial than that recommended by Owen, the Shakers "have prospered and continue to prosper while Mr. Owen's grand experiment in Indiana has resulted in failure."

Hepworth Dixon thought the Shakers had "some singular attractions," but he did not include celibacy among them. Observing the Shaker children at play, he asked, "Is it not sad to reflect that those merry boys and girls whose voices come in peals of laughter down the lane will never if they stay in the community have little ones of their own to play on this village sward?"

The nineteenth-century visitors did not give a complete or detailed account of the economic life of the Shakers. Many of them merely listed the sales items they saw in the society stores. Even so, the lists indicate how quickly the Shakers built their mills and shops, not only to meet their own needs but to turn the surplus into profit.

As early as 1828, the Duke of Saxe-Weimar found he could buy in Shaker shops wooden utensils, sieves, brushes, harness, table linen, coarse silver writing pens, very good rose water, and books about Ann Lee and the Shaker faith. Others mentioned additional items, such as baskets, measures, oval boxes, brooms, knitted wares of every kind, cordage, pin-cushions, woolen cloth, tow linen, palm and feather fans, and bonnets. Ladies' reticules and confectioneries were made particularly for the trade.

Marianne Finch spoke of the applesauce made at Shirley. The community could sell "any quantity of the apple sauce which was put into buckets made by themselves of white wood, holding 2 or 3 gallons each."

Bread, butter, milk and cream, and cheese were all sold. In 1811, 2,884 pounds of cheese were made at Canterbury. Many Clevelanders purchased their fresh dairy products from the North Union peddlers.

Some of the visitors noted the various agricultural products—garden seed, herbs, "vegetable medicines," dried sweet corn, and maple-sugar cakes. The Shakers were the first people to place garden seeds on the market—in the 1790's. Whether the seeds were first marketed by New Lebanon, Enfield,

14 Elder Henry Green, of Alfred, Maine, a man of several abilities, was a member of the ministry. He was also a cabinetmaker who made more than a dozen secretaries and writing desks, as well as numerous sewing desks, for the brethren and sisters, and he was also chief salesman for other Shaker crafts, traveling from hotel to hotel during the summer months. For fifty years he made two trips a year to the White Mountains of New Hampshire and two to the seashore at Rye Beach, New Hampshire, and Kennebunk, Maine, riding his trusty horse many hundreds of miles without accident.

Connecticut, or Watervliet, New York, is not documented, but it is a matter of history that all the Shaker societies raised and packaged seeds for the markets and that this industry was the principal source of Shaker income. Shaker seed merchants made countless trips throughout the countryside on horseback and in their seed wagons. The Ohio salesmen went on western trips, many of them on the Missouri River. The Kentucky salesmen went by boat on the Cumberland, Tennessee, and Mississippi rivers, calling on the merchants along the banks. The return trip from New Orleans was made on the steamboat.

Garden seeds, and also textiles and medicines, were sold on the London market as well as throughout the United States.

By 1820, the Shakers were selling dried roots and herbs. By 1832, they were making extracts. Herb houses were built, and the needed machinery was installed. The New Lebanon and Harvard societies led in the medicinal business in the East, Union Village in the West. In the beginning, the bottled extracts and salves and the boxed powders were sold directly to individuals and private businesses. Later the herbs were dried and shipped to large pharmaceutical firms. For example, in 1889, the Enfield, N.H., brethren shipped some 44,000 pounds of dried dock root to J. C. Ayer and Co., of Lowell, Massachusetts. However, some of the well-established compounds

47

were still marketed by the Shakers themselves—for example, Thomas Corbett's syrup of sarsaparilla.

A late but nevertheless successful enterprise, which lasted well into the twentieth century, was the manufacture of chairs by the South Family at Mount Lebanon, earlier called New Lebanon. An effort was made to produce an article that "could not be surpassed in any respect" and one that combined "all the advantages of durability, simplicity, and lightness." The chairs were produced in sizes from 0 through 7, with the largest weighing only ten pounds.

Another large industry, common to all the societies, was broom-making. Perhaps more Shaker inventions are related to this industry than to any other. The Watervliet, New York, Shakers changed the round broom into a flat one, inventing a press for flattening and holding the straw for stitching. An improved lathe for turning the handles was also invented at Watervliet, and a machine for sizing the broom corn was made at Harvard.

Other articles made by the Shakers for their own use and also for the market were tools, wagons, and carriages, braided horse whips, yarn swifts, carpeting and carpet beaters, and corn planters.

Items of clothing that were sold by one or more societies were linen-bosomed shirts, fur and wool hats, palm leaf and straw bonnets, knitted gloves and sweaters, and cloaks.

The cloak, made and sold at Mount Lebanon, Hancock, and Enfield, Connecticut, was a "handsome, comfortable woman's wrap . . . distinguished in appearance and possessed of excellent wearing qualities." It was advertised to envelop "the whole person, having hood combined for use in storms." For traveling convenience, "it is unequaled on steamers, car or carriage; also an agreeable companion on the mountain and on the seashore." Mrs. Grover Cleveland chose a Shaker cloak for her husband's inaugural. Until recently cloaks for both women and girls could be bought at Canterbury.

Preserved and canned fruit as well as dried fruit brought considerable income, especially in Kentucky. In May 1872, South Union's Church Family alone put up 3,941 jars of cherries and strawberries. June through September would bring plums, quince, damsons, blackberries, and peaches, as well as pears and apples. By the time the demand for the Shaker fruit was greatest, railroad transportation was available, making it possible to ship the heavy wooden cases as far as Texas.

At the two Kentucky societies and at some of the Ohio societies, silk culture was carried on by the sisters. Beginning around 1825 and continuing for approximately fifty years, the Kentucky sisters were quite successful in raising silkworms and weaving silk cloth, most of which was made into

48

15 Sewing room, Mount Lebanon, New York. A catalogue, *Products of Intelligence and Diligence*, published by the Church Family, states: "Making the Shaker cloaks which is an unique and comfortable garment, is one of the principal industries carried on at the present time, and commands large patronage."

kerchiefs. Some of the silk yardage was sold to the eastern Shakers, but usually the extra silk kerchiefs were used as gifts to the eldresses who came as visitors from the eastern societies. A limited quantity of white silk handkerchiefs for men were put on the market at $1.00 each.

All the Shaker societies practiced animal husbandry. Sheep were needed for wool, hogs for meat, and horses and oxen for transportation and in the work program. Dairy and beef cattle were raised. During the periods when as a health measure pork was banned from Shaker tables, hogs were still kept to consume the table waste.

The western Shakers earned the highest reputation as breeders of purebred cattle, usually English Durhams. Many farmers who wanted to start or upgrade a herd did business with the Kentucky and Ohio societies. Before the 1850's, the trustees were selling horses and cattle in Indiana, Illinois, and Tennessee as well as in their immediate areas. With the coming of the railroads, they shipped livestock to Mississippi, Texas, and Kansas.

The society journals contain many entries such as "1832 . . . Our full blooded Durhams are in great demand, but we cannot spare any of them yet." Or ". . . to Nashville to see cattle lately imported from Ireland." The Shakers showed their cattle at both local and state fairs. J. P. MacLean reported that Watervliet, Ohio, took five prizes for cattle in the 1856 fair at Dayton.

From the beginning the Shakers equated work and worship. Good business was good religion. Poor workmanship and dishonest dealing were not tolerated. The trustees were taught that, when selling livestock, it was right to inform the purchaser of any fault or defect in the animal. If the trustees unwittingly cheated anybody, they believed it their duty to make it right. Once, when one of the societies bought some timber and found it more valuable than expected, the trustees voluntarily paid the difference.

It is not surprising that Finch found the nineteenth-century eastern Shakers spoken of in their neighborhood as "honest, truthful, fair-dealing people." She added, "Their out-door deacons are by no means dreamers in their worldly affairs; they know how to make a bargain, always getting the highest prices for their products—which are generally of the best quality."

In the same period, Willis found that every article produced by the Kentucky Shakers "brought a third more in price than any other in the markets of the surrounding towns." He believed this to be right, since "The Shakers raised better vegetables and better cattle than any other class of farmers."

Eldresses Anna White and Leila S. Taylor of Mount Lebanon best defined the Shaker in relation to the world:

> Hardheaded, shrewd, sensible and practical, he neither cheats nor means to let himself be cheated, prefers to give more than the contract demands, glories in keeping the top, middle, and bottom layer equally good in every basket and barrel of fruit or vegetables sent to market under his name.

The eldresses also pointed out that a Shaker "sees no virtue nor economy in hard labor when consecrated brain can work out an easier method." As a result the list of Shaker inventions including "little labor-saving contrivances about the dwellings, shops and barns" is a long one. Few, if any, of the earliest inventions were patented. According to White and Taylor, statistics compiled outside the Order show that "more useful inventions have

50

originated among the Shakers than [among] other people of the same numbers."

Some of the inventions have been: the revolving harrow, Babbitt metal, and the common clothespin at North Union; the screw propeller at Watervliet, New York; a sash balance without cords or pulleys at South Union; machinery for planing, for fertilizing, and for splint-making, basket-making, and box-cutting—all at New Lebanon.

A Harvard sister is credited with being the inventor of cut nails and the circular saw. Abner Bedell of Union Village worked out a large loom for weaving palm-leaf bonnets. Bedell and Thomas Taylor invented a silk-reeling machine that would reel "sixty-three skeins of silk thread in a day." Nelson Chase invented the folding stereoscope at Enfield, New Hampshire. Mowers and reapers were some of the contributions of Maine Shakers.

16 Canterbury Shakers were famous for their baked beans, which were cooked in this revolving oven, a fine example of Shaker ingenuity. In their book *Shakerism*, Eldresses Anna White and Leila S. Taylor wrote: "An invention which has greatly lightened the labors of the sisters who do the family baking is in use at Canterbury. It is a revolving oven, the inner body of the oven having four compartments, each presenting its own door. This is a contrivance of Eldress Emelia Hart, now [1904] of the Ministry of New Hampshire."

Other inventions have been an apple-corer by Sanford Russell at South Union; a one-horse wagon at Enfield, Connecticut, and a dumping wagon at Pleasant Hill; a revolving oven at Canterbury; metal pens by Isaac Youngs of New Lebanon; and machines for printing and filling seed bags and herb packages invented at Watervliet, New York. The first machine for cutting and "bending machine card teeth and punching leather for setting" was invented in New Lebanon in 1793 by Benjamin Bruce. Still other Shaker inventions are a modern kiln for drying sweet corn; a pea sheller; and a "self-acting" cheese press.

Inventiveness as a Shaker characteristic lasted throughout the years. In *The Manifesto* for March 1891, the South Union correspondent wrote:

> One of our members C. Holman has invented a rotary machine and another member Sanford Russell has a steam propeller under way and nearly ready for use. A mania has seemed to take hold of some of the Brothers for inventing and being skillful mechanics, and they are successful.

Then he added, "It is rumored that one of our members is now studying out a plan for a flying machine. If such is the case you may expect a visit from him."

Often the Shaker craftsman took another man's invention and improved on it. For example, the Shaker washing machine that won an award at the Philadelphia Exposition in 1876 was copied and improved with the originator's consent. The Canterbury brethren invented an improved windmill.

Throughout their history, the Shakers were interested in what the outside markets offered that would save them time and increase their production. As soon as steam engines were available, they bought them to replace draft animals. New or improved farm implements, such as threshing machines, clover hullers, and seed separators were examined. If it seemed the new machine would expedite the work, it was purchased. As inventions like the sewing machine, the electric call bell, the telephone, and the automobile came on the market, the trustees bought whatever promised to benefit their business. Shakers were known to have piped water into their dwelling houses and installed hot-air furnaces before such conveniences were found in many of their neighbors' houses.

As long as any Shaker industry was profitable, it was continued, but when it became apparent that a commercial firm could supply "the world" and the societies with an acceptable product at a reasonable price, the trustees admitted the competition, closed their industry, and released the workers for other tasks. The Union Village woolen mill was dismantled in 1869. In October 1871, the South Union society was purchasing cloth in Louisville:

17 Flora Appleton and Fannie Fallon, teachers, with schoolgirls at Enfield, New Hampshire.

"Sisters Sally McComb and Fanny Lacy go with Brother Urban to Louisville. They purchased dark-grounded goods to make the sisters all a dress. Also a new style of woolen fabric denominated Empress goods."

There were always children in the Shaker societies, and they took part in the work program. Some children came into the society with their natural family groups, some with a widowed parent, others as orphans. On occasion parents placed their children with the Shakers to be educated and to learn a trade. In such cases indenture papers were drawn up whereby the Shakers agreed to furnish the children with good wholesome food, with lodging, and with apparel "suitable to the age of the child and to the order of the society."

The Shakers also agreed to teach the children to read and write, "provided they had the capacity to receive such learning." The agreement held only if the Shakers liked the children and the children liked the Shakers. It was made quite plain that the society had no obligation to keep rebellious children.

It was also made clear that when the society took the children it was for the purpose "of making Shakers of them if possible." When the youth reached the age of twenty-one, he had a choice of becoming a covenant member or leaving the society.

It was natural that the boys should work with the men, learning the care of animals, the methods of farming, and the manual skills needed in the various crafts.

The girls were taught the domestic skills. When working in the dining room they were taught never to carry more than six plates or saucers, never more than four cups, and never more than one pitcher, unless the pitchers were empty. There was considerable variety in the girls' work program. In a letter to *The Manifesto*, one girl wrote, "I have been sewing during the past week. I have changed this week to help the sisters sort the winter apples." Another wrote, "Tomorrow is Monday and I think I shall help iron clothes. . . . I am learning to knit. I like to knit the heels better than the toes."

The Shaker leaders always knew the value of tempering work with play—for the adults as well as for the children. In the official journals one can read such entries as, "June 3, 1818. Sandy and all the little boys go to Drakes Creek fishing and for a little pic-nic," or "April, 1837, Casandra and her flock of little girls went out to the cave for recreation and amusement having been confined some weeks platting [straw or palm]."

The children often made their own fun. Hervey Elkins recalled assisting in the gathering of fruit during his Shaker boyhood. "Many a merry sport had we in simulating the modes of Indian warfare, by throwing apples from ambuscades." He also recalled how, during the haying, teams of men and boys "would rival one another by galloping the loaded wagons to the barns."

The school terms were arranged around the work program, with the boys usually going to school during the winter and early spring, and the girls attending classes during the summer and fall. In the early years the subjects were reading and writing, spelling, geography and grammar, and always arithmetic. Later the teachers added history, astronomy, geometry, algebra, and drawing.

Seth Y. Wells of Mount Lebanon, a well-educated and scientific Shaker who had previously taught in Albany schools, went from society to society regulating the school programs. Later the teachers went outside to attend school institutes to learn the recommended educational methods in their states.

Shaker prosperity and growth peaked in the 1850's. By the 1870's a decline was noticeable. Factors contributing to the decline were the Civil War and the subsequent restoration period, the nationwide financial panic of 1873, the widespread shift to commercial steam manufacturing, and the waning interest in communal living, evidenced by the closing of most of the other Utopian societies.

The Civil War affected the eastern Shaker communities to some extent, but the two Kentucky societies were most affected. Located in the border territory where neighbors and even families were divided, these Shakers found it hard to maintain a neutral position. Just as they had been at the time of the Revolution and the War of 1812, the pacifist Shakers were suspect. Their Federal neighbors could not understand their refusal to take up arms. Their southern neighbors resented their abolitionist principles.

The soldiers and officers of both armies soon learned that a Shaker village was the best place to get home-cooked food, forage, and possibly fresh horses. Both Kentucky villages were overrun by military units, and the societies were poorer after each invasion. New fence rails may have been burned as firewood, the fruit orchards robbed, or the horses and wagons "pressed." Then there was the almost daily feeding of military groups, which often numbered in the hundreds.

Many of the military personnel had never heard of the Shakers until they found themselves passing through their villages. Their reactions to the society members differed. A Texas soldier, learning that eighty to ninety people lived in one South Union dwelling house, exclaimed, "If that many soldiers lived in one house they would fight and kill each other. This must be a heaven on earth." But a young officer, angered when he failed to get a fresh horse, said, "You ought to be blowed out and the place destroyed. Here we are going night and day to protect you and what in the name of Hell do you do for your country?"

A captain who knew what it was to be "at war fighting and killing" commended the Shakers for remaining "quietly at home improving their village." The specific improvement was a newly laid stone walk.

The Reconstruction era also created problems for the western Shakers. The financial pinch of the time, followed by the 1873 panic, meant reduced markets. In the period of industrialization and urbanization following the war, the shift from agricultural and individual craftsmanship to industrialism geared to mass production brought rapid change to the Shaker communities. The younger Shakers were attracted to the growing cities. Some of the older but still able-bodied men were drawn to the free government lands in the West. The decreasing Shaker ranks could have been kept up for a time by receiving all the middle-aged and older applicants, but it was apparent that most of these could no longer "give the first fruits of their lives to the communal venture." To protect themselves from receiving members who would be a drain rather than a benefit, the leaders instituted some new membership regulations. About 1902, some societies specified that all applicants must have healthy bodies and be under fifty years of age.

With fewer members coming in and more going out, the time came when there was not enough manpower to farm the extensive lands. As early as

1880, parts of the Ohio Shaker lands were being rented to tenants. Soon all the societies were renting out lands or were hiring men at weekly wages to farm and do other work.

It became apparent to the Mount Lebanon central ministry that some communities should be closed and the property sold. Among these were Tyringham, closed in 1875, North Union in 1889, Groveland in 1892, and Watervliet, Ohio, in 1900. (Busro, or West Union, had already closed in 1827 because of poor health conditions and the upheavals of the War of 1812.) The members of each society that was closed moved to another society, unless they chose to live with or near friends or relatives. All who established themselves outside the society were usually given their proportionate part of the total realized from sale of property.

By 1901 there were less than six hundred members left in the thirteen remaining communities. Four communities would close in the next decade— Whitewater in 1907, Shirley in 1909, and Union Village and Pleasant Hill in 1910.

During the years when the Shaker industries were being terminated, lands being rented out, membership diminishing, and some of the societies closing, it was natural that the older members should be saddened. Many had personal recollections of some of the veteran leaders and had known the communal experiment in the years of its highest accomplishments.

The tone in the journal entries of the time is one of regret: "March 1, 1891, Meetings in the families—The first time that no grown sister stood up to sing—but 4 little girls—oldest 14," and "August 3, Only 3 Brethren dressed in Shaker costumes. How are the mighty fallen!!!"

The reduced membership at South Union is clearly revealed in two 1916 entries: "May 27, Aunt Nancy Sawyers got dinner today, she is hired half of every day to work in the Centre House." And, "May 31, Centre family had their first green beans and peas this year. The sisters bought them in Bowling Green yesterday. This is strange to say."

The time had also come when "6 dozen chairs," a new bedstead, and several coffins were purchased on nearby markets instead of being made by the brothers in the village shops.

But sadness and regret did not give way to despair and inactivity. Realistic and commonsense adjustments were made. The lively marching or dancing in the family meetings diminished because of the decreased membership and the greater ages of most of the members. Worship services were closed to the public. There was consolidation within the individual societies, with two or more families merging and occupying one dwelling house.

Even in the period of decline, new interests were developed. Beginning in

1870, instruction in vocal and instrumental music was introduced at Canterbury. Lectures on the rudiments of music were given by a Boston professor, and classes in correct breathing and tone control were held. Brother N. A. Briggs of Canterbury went to Mount Lebanon, Watervliet, and South Union to introduce singing schools. The societies bought melodeons and pianos. Canterbury installed a pipe organ. Elder Eades, although over seventy, learned to play South Union's new reed organ. In 1958 Eldress Marguerite Frost of Canterbury wrote:

> Music brought much joy to all communities. Community "sings" were occasions to which they looked forward. At Enfield, New Hampshire, some of the brothers formed a string trio. A quartet of talented sisters of Canterbury gave concerts not only for the pleasure of the society but in other towns and cities. Later a small group of sisters in the same community formed an orchestra which provided pleasant relaxation. Another company of sisters at Sabbathday Lake had an interesting orchestra group for some time. . . . Christmas, Easter, and other occasions were opportunities to display any Thespian ability. Young people progressed as they took part in dialogues, plays, and pageants.

18 The New Gloucester Quartet at Sabbathday Lake, Maine. Sabbathday Lake had formerly been known as New Gloucester. This group and the Canterbury Quartet gave concerts not only for Shaker audiences, but also for "the world's people."

The new emphasis on music, elocution, and drama was complemented by advanced instruction in "free-hand drawing, painting, the languages, and bookkeeping."

Sister Helena Sarle, of Canterbury, and Brother Delmer Wilson, of Sabbathday Lake, became accomplished painters. Today their paintings hang at Canterbury and Sabbathday Lake—on walls that once were kept completely bare of decoration.

Some of the sisters turned to creative needlework. Crocheted doilies and antimacassars and covers with crocheted edging or fringe were made and used on chairs, tables, and candlestands. Thus Victorianism began to replace the earlier Shaker simplicity.

Other rules were relaxed. The retiring rooms, once accommodating two or three, now became private rooms where the occupant expressed his or her individuality. One eldress pleasured herself with red flowered curtains; another papered the walls and ceilings of her room so that "her collection of china showed off to advantage." Another sister bought herself a victrola and entertained visitors with her records, evidence that private ownership had supplanted communal holdings.

D. A. Buckingham, a Shaker, testified that Shakers were not averse to change.

> We are not so superstitious in our notions, nor set in our views that we cannot alter when we have become sensible that such change will affect us for good. Progression is one of the prominent points of our religious faith and we endeavor to make it manifest in things spiritual and temporal.

Elder Henry Blinn said, "As the earth or world moves, the people must move with it or be left in the rear." Eldresses White and Taylor spoke of how "in Shakerism the pulse of the spirit is ever replacing old forms by new growth and beauty." To make their point, the eldresses wrote, "The Shaker may change the style of coat, may alter the cut of her gown or cease to wear a cap—and no harm be done." However, in changing her style of dress, no sister went so far as to adorn herself with "birds, wings, or skins," for to do so would have broken with the Shaker practice of kindness to all creatures—human or dumb. No Shaker brother went "about with a murderous gun, speaking death to God's praised singers."

There had been a time when, because land was precious and because raising flowers or other plants for enjoyment was forbidden, only useful plants and trees were grown. But well before the turn of the twentieth century, sisters had their flower gardens and elders could plant and enjoy a magnolia, a holly, or an ornamental pine.

Throughout the nineteenth century, the Shaker societies had received newspapers and magazines, and useful books on many subjects had been purchased. But from 1870 on, a much wider range of reading material was available. Some communities had libraries from which books like Murray's *History of England*, Dr. Rose's *Hints and Helps to Health and Happiness*, and *Light from the Spirit World* could be checked out for reading in one's room or in the "well-lighted, screened-in summer house."

Between January 1871 and December 1899, the Shakers published a society periodical under the editorship of George Lomas and later under that of Elder Henry Blinn and Eldress Antoinette Doolittle. Appearing under four different titles successively—*The Shaker, The Shaker and Shakeress, The Shaker Manifesto*, and *The Manifesto*—the magazine was a means of keeping the scattered societies in contact with one another. Reports from every society appeared in each issue. Also featured were reprints of early Shaker publications, the manuscript journals kept by prominent leaders, and accounts of the early history of each society.

The Shakers who had once sent only their elders and trustees out to do business with "the world" now began to go in groups to attend outside events and to identify with many movements. They participated in a "spiritualistic convention" in Cleveland, attended an 1894 Christian Science meeting in Dayton, and sent delegates to the national conventions of the Peace Movement in the 1890's and early 1900's.

Official journals from after 1870 record trips to attend the lyceum and the Chautauqua, to the Boston Athenaeum, even to see Barnum's show and a medium. The Shakers visited in the homes of their neighbors and friends and went to civic and patriotic meetings.

Times of relaxation within the societies were filled with various activities —learning folk dances; playing checkers, dominoes, flinch, and Parcheesi; working jigsaw puzzles; making popcorn balls and pulling molasses candy; going on picnics and chestnut hunts; and fishing in their ponds. In describing the recreation of the twentieth-century Shakers, Sister Miriam Wall also wrote of "gathering wild flowers while hiking in the woods, playing Ping Pong and tennis, and going coasting and sleigh-riding." The automobile made trips to the mountains and to the seashore possible for the eastern societies.

With the passing of time came the closing of the last western society and six more eastern ones—the Enfield societies in 1917 and 1918, Harvard in 1919, South Union in 1922, Alfred in 1931, Watervliet in 1938, and Hancock in 1959–60.

Today the two remaining societies—Canterbury and Sabbathday Lake— are trying to keep the Shaker torch lighted. In the 1950's, the Canterbury sisters agreed to participate in a series of public seminars and to speak on

Shaker music, inventions, industry, recreation, education, and history. The seminar talks have been printed in pamphlet form. In 1961, the society at Sabbathday Lake began to publish *The Shaker Quarterly*, designed to keep alive the "divine truths upon which Shakerism has rested for nearly two hundred years."

The sisters in both societies—for now there are no brothers—have set up exhibits of Shaker crafts, furniture, and other artifacts. Summer tours are conducted at both villages. Recently Canterbury has restored and opened its schoolhouse, Sabbathday Lake its herb house. Throughout the year the sisters make items to sell in their stores.

Today's student of Shakerism can also visit restored buildings and exhibits at the former villages of Hancock, Massachusetts, and Pleasant Hill and South Union, Kentucky. Several museums and libraries throughout the nation have excellent Shaker collections.

The bicentennial year of the American Shakers—1974—and subsequent years will bring many studies related to Mother Ann's followers, their beliefs and practices, their publications and their handicrafts.

But the clearest image of the Shakers and Shakerism will always be found in the words and photographs of the Shakers themselves. Elder Frederick Evans said, "We are celibates—monks and nuns without bolts and bars." "Shakerism," he declared, "combines science, religion, and inspiration. It is a practical religion." Eldress Dorothy Durgin knew it took "the whole man, the whole woman, to be a Shaker." It was agreed that Shakers are "those who give to God the first fruits of their lives." Elder Blinn said: "Where Shakerism is in operation, there is fulfilled the Lord's prayer." Sister Lillian Phelps, who died in 1973 at the age of ninety-six, could say of herself and other Shakers that "whether engaged in the necessary industries of the home, or in simple recreation, the life of a Shaker is one of contentment, peace, and genuine happiness."

Eldress Marguerite Frost spoke of a Shaker as one who loved "not with a selfish love but with an unwearied love, consecrating and re-consecrating his life and his soul, dedicated to making the Kingdom of Heaven a living, personal reality."

To realize all that was expected and required of a Shaker is to understand Elder Frederick Evans's candid statement: "All men and women cannot be Shakers, nor do we wish them to be."

JULIA NEAL, a native of Kentucky and authority on Kentucky history, recently retired as director of the Kentucky Library and Museum, Bowling Green.

The Shakers in Their Homes

The Shakers' love of home is expressed in many of their writings, in their journals, and particularly in their letters to one another. Always first commenting on the health of the family, they also wrote about conveniences to make labor easier, a freshly painted building, a new roof—all testifying to great pride in their homes and to "Shaker order."

The family unit was a devoted one and ties to other Shaker societies were strong. There was much joyous visiting back and forth, with affectionate welcoming, singing, and special poems for the occasion. Shaker hospitality was bountiful and generously offered. One Ohio community wrote of visiting another:

> When the music ceased, we responded with thankful hearts from which flowed emotions of gratitude better imagined than expressed. We entered the office where we found every possible arrangement for our comfort. We were soon seated at a sumptuous supper which was enjoyed by all to the very last morsel with relish and gratitude. After a refreshing interview with the Elders we retired to rest.

An English traveler, Hepworth Dixon, wrote about Mount Lebanon in particular, but his picture would apply as well to all Shaker settlements from Maine to Kentucky:

> No Dutch town has a neater aspect, no Moravian hamlet a softer hush. The streets are quiet; for here you have no grog-shop, no beer-house, no lock-up, no pound; of the dozen edifices rising about you—work rooms, barns, tabernacles, stables, kitchens, schools, and dormitories—not one is either foul or noisy; and every building, whatever may be its use, has something of the air of a chapel. The paint is all fresh; the planks are all bright; the windows are all clean. A white sheen is on everything; a happy quiet reigns around.

21 North Family kitchen, Mount Lebanon, New York. Note the fly-paper garlands overhead and the large range.

22 The same kitchen a few years later.

23 Sisters sewing at Canterbury, New Hampshire. Note the paneled stove designed by the Canterbury society. The sewing desk at right was designed for maximum work-surface, storage, and general utility. Chairs not in use can be seen hung from pegs in true Shaker fashion. Sisters from left to right are: three whose names are not known, J. E. Wilson, Elmira Hillgrove, Sarah T. Wilson, Jennie Fish, Elizabeth Sterling, Eldress A. Johns, Iona Crooker, unknown, Mary L. Wilson, and unknown.

24 Ironing room in the laundry at the North Family, Mount Lebanon. Brother Daniel Offord, at rear, is using a press to finish napkins and other flat pieces.

25 Mount Lebanon, New York. Young sisters in their sewing room at the Church Family. The room contains many decorations, even a birdcage (pets had been forbidden in the early years), and the sisters wear contemporary hair and clothing styles.

26 Elderly sister and young visitor at Mount Lebanon. Note the beautiful tailoring counter at the right.

27 The winter's supply of wood at Canterbury, New Hampshire. At the time this picture was taken, over four hundred cords of wood were needed each winter by the family for the wood-burning stoves in each room.

28 The South Family's laundry, Enfield, Connecticut. Vat-sized tubs are powered by the line shaft on the ceiling. Handmade buckets are in the foreground. The wooden carrier on the large tub at the left is for wet clothes. The stovepipe on the ceiling heated the room. This is a stereographic view.

29 A stereographic view taken at the Second Family, Mount Lebanon. Oxen draw stone boats on a secondary road in the shop area.

30 Dining room, Middle Family, Mount Lebanon.

At seven o'clock the bell rang for breakfast. The brothers and sisters assembled each by themselves, in rooms appointed for the purpose; and at the sound of a small bell the doors of these rooms opened, and a procession of the family was formed in the hall, each individual being in his or her proper place, as they would be at table. The brothers came first, followed by the sisters, and the whole marched in solemn silence to the dining room. The brothers and sisters took separate tables, on opposite sides of the room. All stood up until each one had arrived at his or her proper place, and then at a signal from the Elder at the head of the table, they all knelt down for about two minutes, and at another signal they all arose and commenced eating their breakfast. Each individual helped himself; which was easily done, as the tables were so arranged that between every four persons there was a supply of every article intended for the meal. At the conclusion they all arose and marched away from the tables in the same manner as they marched to them; and during the time of marching, eating and re-marching, not one word was spoken, but the most perfect silence was preserved.

—John Humphrey Noyes,
History of American Socialisms, 1870

31 The dining room in the dwelling at Canterbury festooned with Christmas wreaths and colorful garlands. Places were set for four—three groups at each table for twelve. Low-back chairs were designed to slide under the tables between meals. Note the large number of built-in cupboards and drawers, for which the Shakers were renowned and which were needed to provide a place for everything and to keep everything in its place.

32 Brethren and sisters standing before the East Family dwelling house of the Hancock Shakers. A carriage-landing can be seen protruding through the fence.

33 The First Family dwelling in Alfred, Maine. Built in 1795, it burned in 1902. The bell on the roof awoke the village in the morning and called the family together for meals; in case of fire, the bells on all the buildings were rung continuously.

34 The old dwelling house built in 1795 at Sabbathday Lake, Maine. The building was demolished in 1882. Amelia stands at the corner of the porch, Mary Curtis is sitting, and Eliza Abbot is standing on the back porch.

35 A postal card showing the workroom at Enfield, Connecticut.

36 Brethren and young sisters at Pleasant Hill, Kentucky. The photograph was probably taken at "the upper farm," which bordered the turnpike to Harrodsburg.

37 Sisters sort cherries at Enfield, New Hampshire.

38 Summer scene at Shirley, Massachusetts.

Their Children—

The Shakers of the Future

39 Summer school at Mount Lebanon, New York. Garlands on the ceiling are fly-paper rings.

ager as they were to increase their number by admitting children and young people into societies, the Shakers' sense of fairness would not let them exert undue pressure to become Shakers on the boys and girls in their care.

The first written covenant, New Lebanon, 1795, specified that a child could not be received as a member and that paternal consent was necessary even before he could be accepted into the society's care. At twenty-one, the young person was free to leave or to remain.

There were strict regulations under "The Children's Order." Girls and boys lived apart from each other and apart from most adults and had special "caretakers," responsible to the elders or eldresses, to look after them.

The education of children under the care of the Shakers was conceded to be superior to that in other rural communities. In some cases, the Shakers

40 Nehemiah White and his boys "farming" at Watervliet, New York. As these boys' "caretaker," he was concerned with every phase of their daily life—both work and play.

41 Schoolgirls with their teacher at Watervliet. The hairnets worn by the girls were replaced by white net caps as they became older.

provided the only school in a district, and non-Shakers attended it. Emphasis was placed on a good practical and moral education and careful training by example and admonition. The reading of suitable books was considered an indispensable "true channel of instruction."

Horace Mann, reformer and advocate of systematic public-school education, once visited relatives in Richmond, Massachusetts, near the Hancock Shakers. The celebrated educator knew that the Shakers, while providing sound elementary-school teaching, had resisted all attempts by the local school committee to supervise the education of the children in their communities, but he did not see how he could persuade the Shakers, who were known for the quality and integrity of all their products, to conform to the educational standards he advocated.

Each Shaker village had its own well-built and completely equipped schoolhouse. An older sister who was the schoolmistress was often assisted by a younger sister. The boys attended school in the winter, and were thus freed to work on the farms in the summer. The girls attended school in the summer with time off to help with kitchen chores during the canning season.

42 Eldress Anna Case (1845–1938), beloved teacher and outstanding leader at Watervliet. Upon her death the Watervliet community closed and its members moved to Mount Lebanon.

43 Eldress Anna Case and her girls.

44 Shaker children and their school at Alfred, Maine.

45 Girls and boys at Mount Lebanon proudly display the fruits of the harvest. Younger girls were all dressed alike, but in less severe garb than that of the older sisters. Boys are in their Sunday best.

46 Mount Lebanon, New York. Maps and charts were permitted on schoolroom walls for teaching purposes and were not regarded as decoration.

47 Canaan, New York. The Upper Family school five miles from the Mount Lebanon community. The girls wore tight hairnets to keep their hair smooth and unruffled.

48 Four young sisters pose on the steps of the Mount Lebanon meeting house. They are members of the reading class in the picture below.

49 Reading class held out of doors at Mount Lebanon, New York, as part of the summer schooling given to girls.

50 Enfield, Connecticut. Young girls in checked pinafores pose with their "caretakers." This early photograph shows the sisters' garb before it was modernized.

51 Enfield, Connecticut. Older sisters caring for little boys and girls.

52 A group of children sitting on the kitchen porch at Enfield, Connecticut.

53 Gymnastic exercises at Canterbury, New Hampshire, were part of the schoolday routine. From left to right are: Marion Montague, Coral Newhall, Gertrude Young, Sarah F. Wilson (the teacher), Jennie H. Fish, Cleora Cashwell, Mary S. Wilson, and Lizzie Fish.

54 Schoolroom at Canterbury, New Hampshire. Very young boys attended classes with girls during the summer. The large broadside served as a teaching aid in elocution lessons.

55 Williams Briggs with a group of his students on the side steps of the dwelling at Canterbury, New Hampshire.

56 Two boys, Henry Mead and Walter Wilson, drinking from a well at Canterbury, New Hampshire. Like the next photograph, this one was obviously carefully posed.

57 "The Young Student" was the title of one of the stereographic views taken at Canterbury, New Hampshire. He was Henry Mead of that community.

58 School at Whitewater, Ohio, in 1897. Pearl McLain, the teacher, is at right in the front. This is probably the only photograph in existence of this school, which was razed soon after 1900.

59 Singing class at Enfield, New Hampshire, with boys on one side and girls on the other. The teacher is leading at the organ. A piano is at the far side of the room. Most of the communities had music rooms where regular singing classes were held.

61 Boys at the well at Enfield Village in New Hampshire.

60 The Church Family schoolroom at Mount Lebanon. Girls are reciting for visiting sisters. Brother Seth T. Welk proposed that "Shaker schools be opened to visitors and strangers, who might wish to inspect the pupils' work."

62 Schoolroom at Mount Lebanon, New York, Left to right are three teachers, Brother James Calver, Sister Amelia Calver, and Sister Emma J. Neale. In the rear is the superintendent, Elder Calvin Reed.

63 Girls of the Church Family at Enfield, Connecticut, in 1886.

PRECEDING PAGE:
64 Pleasant Hill, Kentucky. Sisters are shown about 1890 as they cross the main street of the village from the Centre Family dwelling house on their way into the meeting house. Some of the rules had been relaxed, and at this time brothers and sisters were permitted to enter by the same door.

Shaker meeting houses were used on the Sabbath for the united worship of all the families within each society. The traditional services were held morning or afternoon, sometimes both, and lasted for several hours. The families would march to the church in files of two, the elders in the lead, the sisters following the brethren. The sisters entered the meeting house by the door on the left, the brethren by the one on the right. Typically, the two eldresses and the two elders occupied quarters on the second floor above the meeting room. On the third floor or in an ell were rooms for visiting ministry.

During certain periods when the Shakers wished to be better known and appreciated, the meetings were open to the public. When it was felt that "the world" was showing scorn or ridicule, or creating unpleasant diversions, the meetings were closed.

In Shaker worship, songs, tunes, and dances were inseparable and indispensable forms of expressing religious praise, joy, and aspiration. Although the songs, marches, and other forms of devotional "exercises" were composed by individuals, they were invariably intended for communal use.

The following excerpts from Shaker journals give contemporary accounts of the meetings.

Eldress Betsy Smith, from South Union, Kentucky, visiting Mount Lebanon in 1864, wrote of attending church meeting:

65 Shakers entering the meeting house at Mount Lebanon.

They opened the meeting by singing a most beautiful and Heavenly Hymn then Elder Brother Daniel Crossman made appropriate remarks respecting love for the Western Believers. . . . Then Elder Brother Daniel opened the way for us to deliver the love from the West. . . . We first labored in the square order. Then marched in the circle. Then circular shuffle in a kind of a loop while running round in the first part of the Tune. Had but one quick song—never took our own side of the room for the mixed dance.

Elder Henry Blinn, of Canterbury, in 1873 visited South Union and recorded in his journal a description of worship with that society:

Elder Hervey then reads a letter. Two circles are then formed for the march. The order of this exercise is rather quicker than the N.Y. socieities, but more moderate than some societies. March two songs, sing a select song. Sing two songs for slow march; then two songs for circular dance. Brethren and Sisters now return to their respective sides of the room and have a quick dance. Really we thought the song was without end. . . . One new feature of the meeting was that while marching in the circle, suddenly the Elders whirled around and were marching in the opposite direction between the circles giving out love.

66 A photograph taken by the official photographer of the Poland Spring House, a famous resort hotel, in the late summer of 1883. The only known photograph of a nineteenth-century Shaker meeting, it shows the Church Family of Sabbathday Lake, Maine, in public meeting, with visitors from "the world" occupying the rear benches.

67 The meeting house at North Union (Cleveland), Ohio. It was dedicated November 29, 1848. In his journal of 1848 James Prescott wrote: "Great Day! We commenced laying the foundation of a new Meeting House 100 by 50 feet. All the Brothers have joined hands in this good work. The Sisters have helped in many ways, especially by carrying our meals when it was not convenient to lay down our tools. Only consecrated hands were employed at this task."

68 Shaker sisters leaving the meeting house at Harvard, Massachusetts, 1916.

69 The meeting house at Canterbury was built in 1792 by Moses Johnson, master builder of seven Shaker meeting houses similar in style to this one.

"Consecrated Ingenuity"– *Industry and Agriculture*

71 Lillian Barlow as a young woman.

PRECEDING PAGE:
70 Lillian Barlow (1876–1942), at Mount Lebanon, was the last Shaker to make chairs in any of the societies.

haker historians Anna White and Leila S. Taylor describe the industrious Shakers:

Although claiming to live in the New Heavens, to lead a pure, spiritual and peaceful existence, the Shaker is by no means a dreamer or a mystic. Hard-headed, shrewd, sensible and practical, he neither cheats nor means to let himself be cheated, prefers to give more than the contract demands and glories in keeping the top, middle and bottom layer equally good in every basket or barrel of fruit or vegetables sent to market under his name. He aims to employ his whole being and all his time, consistently and honorably, in the service to which he has devoted himself. He sees no virtue nor economy in hard labor when consecrated brain can work out an easier method. There is no quickener to brain and hand like a heart at peace, a conscience clear and a sense bright with the joy of holy living; and thus the world is richer for many tangible proofs of the Shaker's consecrated ingenuity.

Cloth used for clothing was, at first, woven by the sisters on order from the tailors and tailoresses. Later, quantities of fabric were purchased from "the world" for uniformity of color and texture. The actual making of the sisters' garments was under the direction of the deaconesses in the sewing rooms. The brethrens' clothes were made in the clothiers' shops. At first everything was stitched by hand, but with the advent of the sewing machine, patented by Elias Howe in 1846 and bought in large numbers by the United Society from the Civil War on, the work of making clothing for their large families became much easier.

72 Busy production room of the North Family, Mount Lebanon. A Seth Youngs clock hangs on the wall.

73 Sewing room at Mount Lebanon, New York. Note the wide counters for cutting yard goods.

74 Enfield, Connecticut. Harriet Offord is spinning at the wool wheel.

75 The "Dorothy" cloak was named for Eldress Dorothy Durgin, of Canterbury, New Hampshire. She perfected the design and saw to its manufacture.

77 Anna Delcheff, a Hancock sister, poses proudly in her lovely cloak.

76 Sabbathday Lake, Maine. Left to right: Sarah Fletcher, Laura Barley, Lizzie Barley, Eldress Prudence Stickney, Clara Chase, Viola Daniels, Iona Sedgelay.

78 Bertha Mansfield, Canterbury, New Hampshire, is weaving poplar sheets, which were cut and shaped into the sisters' bonnets. She is shown using a Shaker-built two-harness loom. Woven poplar was also used to make sewing boxes and other notions. Palm leaf was also used for bonnets.

79 Deaconesses' sewing room showing sisters making cloaks and bonnets at Mount Lebanon.

80 Enfield, Connecticut. Two sisters weave rugs. Elder George Clark is at left.

81 Shaker boxes are probably the best known of all Shaker products. These carriers, shown with Brother Delmer Wilson of Sabbathday Lake, had maple sides and pine bottoms. Boxes were shaped under steam around oval forms. The distinctive "fingers" reached down the side of each box and were fastened with minute copper nails. Carriers were made both with and without covers; many were finished by the sisters, who lined them with silk to make them into sewing boxes. This picture shows the product of a commendable season's work, totaling 1,083 pieces.

82 Canterbury, New Hampshire. Edna Fitts, Elizabeth Martin, and Mary Louisa Wilson are molding maple-sugar cakes. Northern communities all had extensive "sugar bushes," and the syrup from these groves was the basis of a lucrative business. The making of maple-sugar cakes, sometimes with butternuts, was a busy seasonal activity.

The earliest evidence describing chair-making as a Shaker industry was a note in Joseph Bennet, Jr.'s daybook. At New Lebanon on October 21, 1789, he recorded the sale of three chairs to Elizah Slosson for eleven shillings. The three-slat, or "common," chair was made in each community for its own use, and many societies also made chairs for sale to "the world."

Lewis & Conger of New York placed large orders for chairs from 1868 to 1875, in which year the cost of chairs they bought amounted to $1,383.28. In that year, rockers with arms were selling for $3.25 for the number 0 model and $8.00 for the number 7. With rockers only, the chairs sold for $3.00 for number 0 to $7.50 for number 7, the largest.

83 The chair shop of the South Family at Mount Lebanon did a brisk cash-and-carry business.

84 Three societies—Mount Lebanon, New York; Enfield, Connecticut; and Union Village, Ohio—claimed the honor of having originated the seed business. D. Clinton Brainard, of Mount Lebanon, conducted that society's garden-seed business, which had begun in the 1790's. The business was a natural undertaking for a farm-and-shop-oriented society which, after providing for its large communities, sold the surplus. The Shakers were the first to sell seeds in paper packages and to control the quality they offered.

85 Of the many Shaker industries, none was more successful from its inception than the botanical medicine business. Roots, herbs, and vegetable extracts for medicinal purposes were placed on the market in the early 1800's. This photograph shows the bottling of medicine at Mount Lebanon, New York.

86 Brother Alonzo Hollister, Mount Lebanon, New York. He was a skillful botanist and chemist and conducted the manufacture of herbal medicines. Here, he sits beside the same kind of vacuum pan that was later adapted by Gail Borden to the making of evaporated milk.

87 The grist mill at North Union, Ohio, was novel and bold in both design and engineering. Built completely of stone with three stone runs, the imposing structure rested upon a solid ledge of rock. The sharp rise from basement to ridge above provided between forty and fifty feet of headwater. The fume, or headstock, was hewn out of solid stone, with its two ends dovetailed into the rock to prevent it from breaking out.

88 Broom factory at Pleasant Hill, Kentucky. Broom corn was grown in large amounts in all the communities, but the Shakers at Watervliet are credited with being the first to raise it and undertake the manufacture of brooms. Theodore Bates of that community is believed to have invented the flat broom.

89 The Hancock Shaker Grist Mill was a well-known institution in Berkshire County, Massachusetts, for almost 100 years. There the Shakers produced flour and feed both for themselves and for their neighbors. The mill was enlarged in 1867 to accommodate three stone runs for milling. Located in West Pittsfield near the terminus of the Pittsfield Electric Street Railway, the mill was a familiar sight to travelers such as these of about 1910.

90 The grist mill at Pleasant Hill, Kentucky, was built alongside the Shawnee Run Creek in 1816-17. With its great overshot waterwheel, it served the Shaker community until the end of the nineteenth century. It was powered by water until 1884, when a steam engine was introduced as more efficient. At left are the remains of the stone oil mill, which made linseed oil by pressing flaxseed. Also powered by water, its wheel can be seen on the left.

91 The blacksmith, an important and permanent part of every Shaker village—indeed of every eighteenth-, nineteenth-, and early twentieth-century village—was often the mainstay of the community's smooth operation, providing assistance to the deacons and deaconesses as a metal fabricator, inventor, veterinarian, and odd jobber. Dan Perole of the Pleasant Hill society is seen here at his forge, which was set up in 1878 near the West Family dwelling house.

92 John Cummings, a trustee at Enfield, New Hampshire, was also a machinist, mechanic, and inventor.

93 Levi Shaw, a trustee of the North Family, Mount Lebanon, manufactured rug beaters.

94 A postcard view of the office and store at Enfield, New Hampshire. The store in a Shaker community was a very busy place. In 1843, the Enfield trustees reported: "Our manufactures are woodenware, such as tubs, pails, half-bushel and other measures, boxes, etc.; also whips, corn-brooms, leather, and various other articles."

95 Sisters in charge pose on the steps of the office and store at Mount Lebanon.

96 The production of adequate supplies of cordwood for the long New England winters filled the days of the Shaker brethren from late summer through fall, once harvesting had been completed. Photographed in 1910 at Sabbathday Lake, Maine, with their eight-horsepower gas-powered buzz saw, are John Pine (sawing), John Darrington (throwing away), Frank Carpenter (hired man), and Heran Bailey (second from left).

To keep the far-flung communities in touch with each other, and perhaps as a way of presenting their image to "the world's people," in 1871 a monthly newspaper, *The Shaker*, began to be published in a quarto form of eight pages. It was under the management of Brother George A. Lomas, of Watervliet, New York. The name was changed in 1873 to *The Shaker and Shakeress*, and it was then edited by Elder Frederick W. Evans and Eldress Antoinette Doolittle, of Mount Lebanon, New York. Lomas again took charge of the paper in 1876, when the name was changed back to *The Shaker*. In 1878, the publication adopted the name *The Shaker Manifesto*, and its form was changed to an octavo of twenty-eight pages. In 1882, the editorial management was moved to Canterbury, New Hampshire, under Henry C. Blinn, and the following year the name was changed again to *The Manifesto*. Although publication of this paper ceased in 1899, the Shakers at Sabbathday Lake, Maine, continue to write today, publishing *The Shaker Quarterly*, first issued in 1961.

97 Brother George A. Lomas, editor of *The Shaker*, in his printing office at Watervliet, New York. A broadside advertising the paper is at the left.

98 Henry Clay Blinn's printing office at Canterbury, New Hampshire. Note the book of typefaces from the Boston Type Foundry.

99 Sister Rosetta Cummings and Sister Henrietta Spooner in the sewing room at Enfield, New Hampshire.

100 Girls of the Canaan Upper Family weave palm leaf while a very young girl knits.

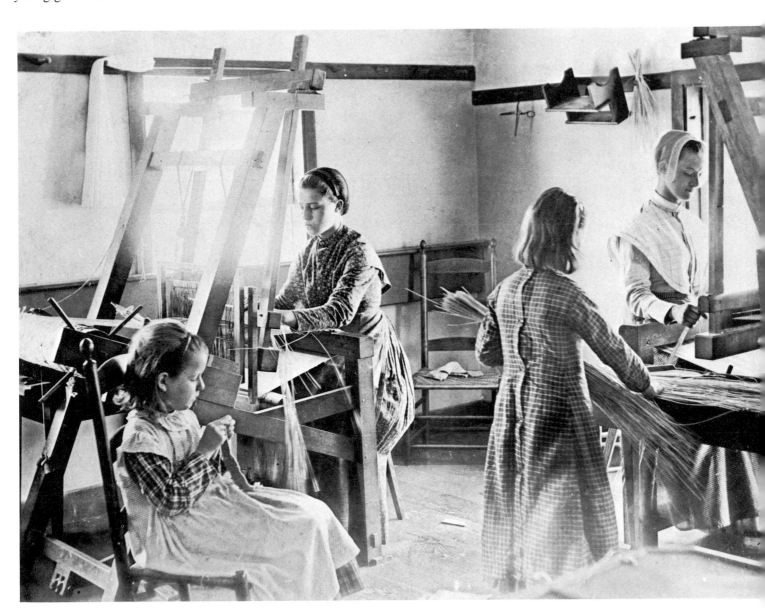

101 The United Society produced many notable examples of architecture, but none more famous than the round stone dairy barn built in 1826 at the Hancock community. Of stone for permanence and in circular form for maximum utility, this building stands three stories high and measures 270 feet in circumference. It could accommodate fifty-two head of cattle and two span of horses, not to mention 300 tons of hay. In 1864, the barn burned completely; only the stone walls were left standing. Rebuilt that same year with the addition of a circular manure pit, the barn was further improved in the 1880's by the addition of the large monitor roof.

In the photograph, boys and brethren milk the herd in the front barnyard.

Agriculture and horticulture, the foundation of all the societies, produced for the Shakers a quality of life outstanding for the time. It supplied their own needs, and the surpluses were sold, thereby producing a steady income. In Shaker farming operations, no pains were spared. Fields were carefully cultivated, and forests used as crops were treated with an eye to conservation and replanting. The Shakers kept fine stock, and Shaker barns were admirably arranged to save labor.

As a matter of principle, the Shakers used the most up-to-date and efficient farm machinery available. They would often redesign machinery they had just bought, adding their own improvements to make it more efficient.

Primarily, their field crops were wheat, rye, oats, corn, barley, timothy, alfalfa, potatoes, and flax, with tobacco in the South and along the Connecticut River.

Every society had vast fruit orchards. The Englishman Hepworth Dixon, writing about his visit to Mount Lebanon, said:

> This morning I have spent an hour with Frederick [Evans] in the new orchard, listening to the story of how he planted it. . . . "A tree has its wants and wishes," said the Elder, "and a man should study them as a teacher watches a child, to see what he wants. If you love the plant and take heed of what it likes, you will be well repaid by it. . . . Now when we planted this orchard, we first got the very best cuttings in our reach; we then built a house for every plant to live in, . . . we drained it well; we laid down tiles and rubble, and then filled in a bed of suitable manure and mould; we put the plant into its nest gently, . . . and protected the infant tree by the metal fence."

The Shakers were famous for their applesauce, pickled pears and cherries, dried peaches and corn. Their preserved products were sold widely, as far west as the Mississippi and as far south as Louisiana.

One writer, summing up an article about the Shakers in the Pittsfield *Sun* for August 14, 1834, stated:

> The great rule of domestic economy, a place for everything and everything in its place, is no where more strikingly exemplified—and tho' they make no pretensions to the fine arts, and have little of what is called taste, yet all their arrangements and the products of their labor exhibit the proofs of thoroughness, permanency, utility, and substantial comfort.

102 On this photograph is written: "Br. Levi Shaw of North Family, Mount Lebanon, N.Y. Arranging to buy the first Harvesting machine ever used in the township, and we have heard, the first one in Columbia Co. N.Y."

103 Anna Case husking corn with her girls at Watervliet. The sisters ran a profitable industry in the sale of dried corn.

104 Sisters at Harvard, Massachusetts, load the cart with the noonday meal for brethren in the fields.

105 Shirley, Massachusetts, barnyard scene. The cart-driver is shown with four yoke of oxen and the lead horse.

106 The great stone barn of the North Family, Mount Lebanon, was completed in 1858 under the supervision of Elder George Wickersham, its designer. The barn was 196 feet long and 50 feet wide, with five floors, three of which could be entered by doors that opened at their level on the hillside, eliminating the need for bridges.

108 A sister making butter at Hancock, Massachusetts. The dairy produced fine butter, which was sold in nearby Pittsfield. Shaker cheese fetched twenty-five cents a pound when that of other farmers brought only seven cents.

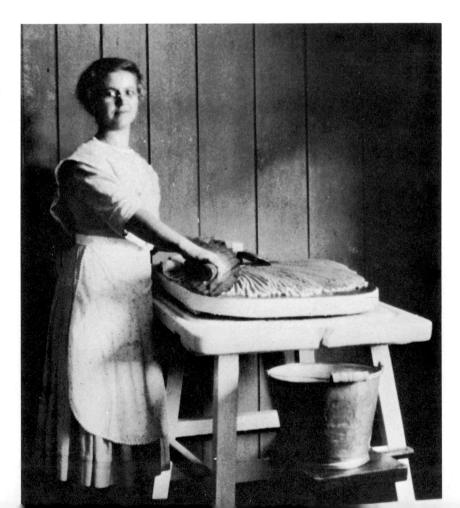

107 Shirley, Massachusetts. Brothers lined up with teams. Buckboards, express wagons, and farm carts were all important farm vehicles.

109 Canterbury, New Hampshire. Young brethren show one of their prize oxen.

110 Dairy at Canterbury. The calendar on the wall fixes the date in August of 1915. The butter-churn is operated by the line shaft, and in the small vat on the stove milk is heated for making cheese.

111 Canterbury, New Hampshire. Ox teams. Twelve yoke of oxen were maintained by this society.

112 Sister Mary and two small Shakers in the flower garden at Canterbury. One wonders at the presence of the drummer-boy, but this photograph was again part of a set of stereographic views made by the photographer as a profit-making venture.

113 Elder Henry Clay Blinn of Canterbury with his beehives. Apiaries are an important element in fruit-farming. The orchards at Canterbury were extensive, and the by-product, honey, was readily marketed.

Shaker
Leaders

PRECEDING PAGE:

114 Henry Clay Blinn entered the Canterbury society of his own accord as a boy of fourteen. An inspiring teacher, editor, author, and printer, he was also a talented botanist and skillful dentist. This outstanding leader was greatly respected not only in every Shaker community, but also in "the world."

Elder Henry in 1899 revised and edited *Gentle Manners, A Guide to Good Morals,* which had been written in 1823 by instructors at the Shaker school in New Lebanon. In his preface to the third edition, he wrote:

> In the education of children and youth, and even of those of more advanced age, there are certain rules of discipline which should be carefully maintained. Our lives are, primarily, for the happiness of those around us with this responsibility. The education of the mind, so essential for the comfort and pleasure of those with whom we associate, now becomes an imperative duty. It is the stepping-stone to a well-ordered Christian life, and harmonizes beautifully with the accepted motto, that, "Order is heaven's first law."

115 James S. Kaime.

Leadership within the Shaker Church was modeled on the character of Ann Lee, the spiritual organizer and first great leader of the Shaker Society in America. She died in 1784, and her physical image was never captured in a visual medium, but she has been vividly portrayed for us in the written testimony of her loyal followers.

In *A Summary View of the Millennial Church,* published in 1823, Calvin Green and Seth Y. Wells, prominent writers of the United Society, described their leader thus:

> Mother Ann was very remarkable, not only for her humility, charity and zeal to do good; but also for her temperance, sobriety, industry, prudence, and good economy. Being herself wholly devoted to the cause of God, she was ever faithful in her endeavors, both by precept and example, to plant the same good qualifications in her followers; so that in all things, she was a pattern of godliness, and showed herself to be a Mother indeed, in every good word and work.

Once established as the criteria for leadership, these qualities permeated all positions of responsibility. Whether male or female, those of the United Society selected to lead or direct had to be "blameless characters, faithful, honest and upright, clothed with the spirit of meekness and humility, gifted with wisdom and understanding, and of great experience of the things of God."

Within each society there were three main kinds of leadership. At the top were the ministers of the society, whose primary function was the overall spiritual and temporal guidance of their respective communities. Next came the elders and eldresses, usually two of each sex, who acted as spiritual leaders and overseers of daily communal life for the family of which they were members. At the bottom of the hierarchy of leadership within the United Society were the deacons and deaconesses, who headed the numerous departments, trades, and businesses in each family. "Office deacons"—more commonly known as "Trustees"—were a specialized branch of this last category and handled all legal and monetary matters and matters dealing with "the world's people." All leaders, no matter what their position, were required to carry on some manual occupation in addition to performing their official duties.

116 Elders, left to right: James S. Kaime (1820–1894), Canterbury, New Hampshire; Abraham Perkins (1807–1900), Enfield, New Hampshire; Henry Clay Blinn (1824–1905), Canterbury; in the rear: Benjamin H. Smith (1829–1899), Canterbury.

These elders epitomize the leadership of the Shakers. Their strength of character, constant good judgment, and dedication to the care of the members in their communities was reflected in the growth and success of their societies. They were "wholly devoted to the cause of God."

117 Benjamin H. Smith.

118 Abraham Perkins.

Conant = Portland.

There were two societies in Maine—at Alfred and at Sabbathday Lake. The last of the eastern societies to be organized—in 1794—Sabbathday Lake will also be one of the last to close. Eight sisters live there today, still maintaining the buildings, conducting their shop, and opening parts of their village to the public each summer.

119 Elder John Bell Vance (1833–1896), of Alfred, had a deep interest in young people and always maintained a large order of boys and young brethren—often so many that there was no need to hire any outside help. Elder Otis Sawyer wrote of John Vance that he was placed in the Elders' Order in the Gathering Family before he was twenty. Vance took a leading part in public meetings, and his talents as a public speaker developed to such an extent that he undertook public lectures on the Shakers in such cities as Portland, Boston, New York, Troy, and Lynn.

120 Elder Otis Sawyer (1815–1884), of the Sabbathday Lake ministry, was a beloved spiritual leader and good businessman, under whose guidance the Maine communities grew and prospered. He lived at Sabbathday from the age of seven and in his youth knew and talked with people who had traveled far to see Mother Ann Lee with their own eyes. These people were some of those who sailed on *The Shark* from a Maine port to New York and thence up the Hudson River to the neighborhood of Albany, near Watervliet. They arrived there in August 1784, a month before Mother Ann's death. Satisfied that she was what she said she was, they returned to Maine to found Shaker communities.

121 Eldress Aurelia Mace (1835–1910), of Sabbathday Lake. It was she who, in the summer of 1900, mistook Charles Tiffany, a guest at the nearby Poland Spring House, for an unemployed tramp. With the generosity characteristic of the Shakers, Eldress Aurelia gave him food, made him lemonade, and brushed off his clothes. The president of the well-known New York store had merely lost his way.

In 1899, Eldress Aurelia wrote *The Aletheia—Spirit of Truth*, a series of letters setting forth the principles of the United Society and the history of the Shakers—principally at Sabbathday Lake—with contemporary illustrations and some poetry.

122 Elder William Dumont, of Sabbathday Lake, was in charge of the herb department, including production of the famous tamar laxative, a fruit compound which he personally took to druggists all over the state, giving them samples and explaining the formula. He was also a famous agriculturist, enormously increasing the productivity of Shaker farms.

123 Eldresses Eliza Smith and Fannie Casey, of Alfred, kept family finances at a favorably high level.

124 Elder Elijah Myrick (1834–1890), of Harvard, Massachusetts, was a talented businessman and craftsman, stone-cutter and spiritual leader, who acted on behalf of his own community and Shirley in matters which often involved the New Hampshire and Maine societies also.

125 Elder Simon T. Atherton (1803–1888), of Harvard, was a trustee who built up the herb and seed industry.

126 Elder Ezra Newton, of Harvard. This photograph was taken on May 23, 1893, three years before Elder Ezra's death at the age of 101.

127 Elder John Whitely, head of the ministry of the communities at Harvard and Shirley, Massachusetts, was born in England. He came to America as a youth, joined the Shakers, and spent his life with them.

128 Eldress Eliza Babbitt (1781–1865), of the Harvard community, was the niece of Tabitha Babbitt—inventor, the Shakers claimed, of the circular saw.

129 A Harvard sister who has been unidentified through the years. Clara Endicott Sears asks, "Is this Leoline?" She thought this pretty sister might be the author of several love sonnets written at Harvard in the 1870's and 1880's and signed merely "Leoline."

In her *Gleanings from Old Shaker Journals*, Miss Sears published one of Leoline's sonnets, written in October 1880.

If I should send a ship to sea to-night
Full freighted with rich stores of uncoined gold,
And bound for India's clime or Iceland's cold—
With floating pennons waving fair and bright—
But with no rudder at the helm to guide—
No white sails waiting to unfurl and fold—
No massive anchor my brave ship to hold—
How could I hopeful be and with heart light
Expect in safety she would reach the other side?
My young heart is a vessel launched abroad
Filled with ambitions, with high hopes and pride—
But without friends, its voyage is a fraud—
True friends to lead, those whom the sea hath tried,
Firm friends, to hold it in the port of God!

an impression as they. Eldress Antoinette and Elder Frederick were among the many Shakers who were strict vegetarians.

Frederick W. Evans, an Englishman by birth, came to the United States with his brother George, Robert Dale Owen, and other reformers. He was a free thinker, a radical, and a materialist and was "surprised that the expression of his infidel sentiments did not seem to disturb the Shakers." That it did not is evidenced by his being permitted to render distinguished service as an elder of the North Family for fifty-seven years. He was a forceful speaker on behalf of the Believers and a prolific author. Although he was a bulwark of Shakerism for so long, he was never asked "to take the head," probably because he was so outspoken on questions of worldly affairs. "We are," he said, "living in a world of ideas. Napoleon

130 Anna White, Antoinette Doolittle, Frederick W. Evans, and Daniel Offord, four outstanding leaders at Mount Lebanon, New York, were recognized throughout the societies for their capability and administrative strength.

Eldress Anna was co-author of *Shakerism: Its Meaning and Message*, a history of the Shakers published in 1904. It was she who, at the age of 75, went to Washington to present President Theodore Roosevelt with the resolutions adopted at the Shaker Peace Conference, August 8, 1906. It was reported that the President gracefully conversed with Eldress Anna and Sister Sarah Burger and that his eyes never wavered from the Eldress's face, nor did her gaze flinch from his steady piercing look. It was, as someone at the time said, "Turk meet Turk."

Eldress Anna was active in reform movements, a member of the National American Woman Suffrage Association, and vice president of the National Council of Women. The North Family, under her leadership for several years, started a branch of the latter organization.

Eldress Antoinette united with the Shakers of her own choice at the age of fourteen. It has been said of her and Frederick Evans that perhaps no one of the outstanding leaders of the last half of the nineteenth century left so strong and lasting

131 Elder Frederick W. Evans.

said in his day the next war would be a war of ideas; how much more does it apply to this, our day!"

Daniel Offord, also born in England, was brought into the Shakers by his father as a boy of 13. By careful study of the scientific journals, he developed his unusual mechanical gifts and became so skilled that he could do nearly all the plumbing, steam-fitting, and machine work for the family. The reservoir at Mount Lebanon, which was constructed in 1876 and had pipes connecting with a distant pond to bring water to dwellings, barns, and laundries, was largely his work. Elder Daniel was head of the North Family for many years. He was a confirmed vegetarian and had a great interest in Christian Science. It is said that to the end of his life he continued to study Mary Baker Eddy's *Science and Health*.

132 Elder Daniel Offord.

133 Eldress Antoinette Doolittle.

134 Eldress Anna White.

135 Mary Whitcher, of Canterbury, New Hampshire, wrote the earliest cookbook in Shaker literature and was the first to give bills of fare—menus for each day of the week. Her book offered 150 nutritious recipes for preparing a variety of fresh natural foods. Called *Mary Whitcher's Shaker House-Keeper*, the book was first published in Boston in 1882. In accordance with the custom of the day, it was not sold, but was given to those interested in the Shaker medicines advertised in it.

In the preface Sister Mary wrote: "The Shakers recognize the fact that good food properly cooked and well digested is the basis of sound health. . . . Sincerely hoping that this unpretentious book may prove generally acceptable to those who love their homes, I remain, yours kindly."

136 Ira Remington Lawson (1834–1905), a noted leader and trustee of the Hancock society, guided its growth for many years. He enlarged its West Pittsfield mills, raised large herds of cattle, and furthered the development of iron-ore mines on the community's property.

137 A Victorian photograph taken in Boston of the Canterbury and Sabbathday Lake Shaker sisters, many of whom became distinguished leaders. Left to right:

FRONT ROW: Elizabeth Haskel. Jesse Evans. Ada Cummings.

SECOND ROW: Sarah Fletcher. Aurelia Mace, Canterbury eldress and author of "The Aletheia."
Dorothy Durgin (1825-1898), of Canterbury, a gifted teacher, eldress, and the author of hymns and anthems, many of which were published. Jenny Fish.

BACK ROW: Prudence Stickney, a trustee and eldress of Canterbury and of Sabbathday Lake, where she died in 1950, aged 90.
Cora Helena Sarle, artist, who, under Elder Henry C. Blinn's direction, did watercolor drawings of the wild flowers and herbs of Canterbury. Josephine Wilson.
Amanda Stickney, Prudence's older sister, of Sabbathday Lake.

138 Sister Martha Jane Anderson
(1844–1897), of Mount Lebanon, who, in her
devotion to hand labor, fulfilled Mother
Ann's famous injunction: "Hands to work
and hearts to God." She was also a vigorous
thinker and writer and contributed regularly
to Shaker publications and local newspapers.
She wrote hundreds of songs and hymns and
had a rare, sweet singing voice.

139 Eldress Harriet Bullard during the early
1900's was head of the central ministry at
Mount Lebanon.

140 Alonzo Hollister (1830–1911), a noted trustee in the Church Family at Mount Lebanon, was in charge of the medicinal herb department.

141 Elder Giles B. Avery, of Mount Lebanon, was a dedicated leader, insistent upon strict adherence to Shaker doctrine. Like many in the ministry, he traveled almost continuously, visiting every community annually. His trip to the Shaker village at South Union, Kentucky, at the height of the Civil War in June 1862, was much appreciated by the Believers there, whose lives were disrupted by both sides in the conflict.

142 George M. Wickersham, of Mount Lebanon, designed and supervised the construction of the great barn at that community. Completed in 1858, it was a mammoth structure 196 feet long and 50 feet wide with five floors in all. It was destroyed by fire September 28, 1972.

143 Sister Emma J. Neale (1857–1943), seated, and Sister Sarah Neale (1849–1948), standing.

The Neale sisters were two of the best-known members of the Mount Lebanon community. Sister Emma served as a trustee for 61 of her 87 years. Her name appears as maker on the labels of many of the beautiful Shaker cloaks.

Sister Sarah lived first at Mount Lebanon, but later moved to Watervliet, New York, where she became a teacher and helped with the newspaper. Returning to Mount Lebanon, in 1898 she was appointed postmistress for the community and served until the post office was closed in 1931.

145 Sister Sarah Neale.

144 Sister Emma Neale.

The Shaker community at Union Village, Ohio, was about halfway between Dayton and Cincinnati. It was the largest Shaker society in the West, second only to Mount Lebanon among the eighteen. In the Irish famine of 1846–47, Union Village sent 1,000 bushels of corn to Ireland, and in the depression following the panic of 1873, it served over 4,300 meals to the hungry poor.

146 Elder Joseph Slingerland, of Union Village, was in charge, in the 1890's, of the remodeling and modernization of the Trustees' Office, or Administration Building, which came to be known as Marble Hall because of his profligate use of seven different kinds of colored marble in the floors and staircase. The result was totally un-Shaker in its lack of simplicity and was such an extravagant piece of folly that the community was forced into bankruptcy.

147 Moore S. Mason, of Union Village, was in charge as a trustee when the village was sold in 1912. Lebanon, Ohio, home of the Lebanon National Bank advertised on the calendar, was the city nearest to the Shakers in Warren County. The Shakers marketed their produce in Lebanon and in Cincinnati and often used the Ohio River to transport goods.

148 Oliver C. Hampton (1815–1901), of Union Village, the author of many poems and odes, was a prolific contributor to *The Shaker Manifesto*.

149 Eldress Clymena Miner (1832–1916), of North Union, Ohio, entered the Society when she was six years old. She grew up with the community (near Cleveland) and shared in its golden age when it numbered two hundred members. She was painstakingly trained at the little brick schoolhouse, became a fine bookkeeper, and sang with spirit and understanding. In 1852, she became a deaconess and within eight years was appointed eldress. Her capable shoulders carried the burden when the community dwindled to twenty-seven members. J. P. MacLean, in his *Shakers of Ohio*, wrote, "Clymena was as pleasant a person as one could meet; she was well informed and was an excellent conversationalist."

CABINET PORTRAIT.
WASHBURY. LOUISVILLE, KY.

150 Elder Hervey Eades (1809–1892), of South Union, Kentucky, was a noted teacher and the author of *Shaker Sermons*, containing the substance of Shaker theology. George A. Lomas, the Shaker editor, called him "a most excellent representation of what Shaker principles can do for a man."

151 Eldress Sarah Ann Collins (1855–1947), of Mount Lebanon, was brought to the Shakers as an orphan at the age of eight. Living with the South Family, she came to head that family as eldress for over sixty years and directed the famous Shaker chair industry which had been started by Robert Wagan.

152 Mother Rebecca Jackson, leader of a Shaker family in Philadelphia whose members were mostly black.

153 Elder William Wilson, of Enfield, New Hampshire, in a photograph taken December 16, 1891. Figure 3 is an early tintype of Elder William.

Mingling with "the World's People"

PRECEDING PAGE:
154 A group of Shakers from the North Family, Mount Lebanon, attended a spiritualist camp meeting at Lake Pleasant, Massachusetts, August 18, 1880.

Clara Endicott Sears, living for many years near the Shakers at Harvard, Massachusetts, became their friend and confidante. In 1916, in *Gleanings from Old Shaker Journals*, she wrote:

The wall of reserve and inaccessibility with which the Shakers have surrounded themselves has made it well-nigh impossible before now to penetrate beyond a certain point into the mysteries of their industrious lives, so intricately interwoven with mysticism and the practice of almost perpetual adoration. But the old antagonism between them and "the world" has long since died away, and the religious excesses of the old days which caused such panic of fear and superstition would be as foreign to the modern Shakers as they would be to any outside of their faith. In the towns surrounding their villages they are regarded as peaceful, honest citizens, and are held in affectionate esteem.

Actually, quite a while before 1916, Shakers were becoming more visible and were receiving guests on many and varied occasions, as these photographs show.

155 Interior of the sisters' store, North Family, Mount Lebanon. Notice the rack of photographic views and postcards of Shaker scenes at the right.

156 In every community the sisters conducted the store, where they sold their beautifully made sewing boxes, dolls, dusters, knitted articles, rugs, fans, pincushions, and other handmade notions.

157 They were justly proud of their handicrafts and candies.

158 In 1903, state officials dined at the North Family at Mount Lebanon. Forty people attended, among them Massachusetts Govern[or] George Nixon Briggs, at left. Also in attendan[ce] at center wearing the hat, is ex-Governor W. Murray Crane, who was elected to the United States Senate the following year. Shakers did [not] vote, but they obeyed the laws and paid taxe[s].

159 Elder Daniel Offord speaks to the visiting Salvation Army members.

160 The Salvation Army visited the North Family at Mount Lebanon and gave a concert.

161 A Peace Conference was held at Mount Lebanon on August 31, 1906. Those attending are shown arriving in both horse carriage and horseless carriage. The public was invited to attend the Conference and did, in large numbers.

162 Chairs set up inside the meeting house at Mount Lebanon in preparation for the Peace Conference.

163 Eldress Anna White is shown addressing the Peace Conference. There were numerous other speakers, many of national reputation, but the most absorbing moment of the day occurred when Eldress Anna stood up at the opening of the afternoon session and read her address in a clear and resonant voice. In part, she said:

From far and near, known and unknown, we make you welcome to this rich feast of intellectual and spiritual thought. You have responded most nobly to our call; a call that arises from a necessity, a call that is being heard increasingly in the earth even as the rolling thunder in these mountain lands increases in volume, as it resounds from valley to hilltop. . . . You may think that, cloistered as we are from the outside world, pursuing the even tenor of our ways, the larger affairs of life, those pertaining to country and nation and not directly affecting us, would not enlist our sympathy nor engage our attention. It is far otherwise. No citizen is more thoroughly alive to the interests of state or nation than are the Shakers. In the Peace of the nation is our Peace.

164 Upon the closing of the South Union, Kentucky, community, five thousand people gathered on September 26, 1922, for the sale of the land, buildings, and furnishings at public auction. South Union was the last of the western communities to disband.

165 It was the sad duty of two elders from the East—Walter Shepard of Mount Lebanon and Arthur Bruce of Canterbury—to supervise the sale.

166 A large group of "world's people" from Auburn, Kentucky, are pictured visiting Shakertown at South Union, Kentucky, in 1911 when the community was still flourishing.

167 The "Rural Home" with its forty rooms was built by Augustus Grosvenor of the Harvard Shakers. Following its completion, the Harvard Shakers, with the help of the Shirley Shakers, paid off a debt of $25,000 on the building. The Rural Home had the Shakers' generous endorsement, but was operated as a well-run summer boarding-house—and not, as some supposed, by the Shakers themselves.

168 On June 30, 1878, these people from "the world" attended a Shaker service at Canterbury, New Hampshire.

Posing for "the World"

PRECEDING PAGE:
169 Brothers and sisters at Watervliet, New York.

170 On the front steps of the brick dwelling house in Hancock, Massachusetts.

As the nineteenth century drew to a close, the Shakers prepared to enter the twentieth presenting the image of their societies in a progressive light. Their well-kept, affluent villages, their successful businesses, and their forward-looking plans for the future belied the fact that membership was declining.

Feeling the need to recruit, but never forgetting that their primary purpose was religious, they rejected many ideas advanced by outside friends who wanted to see Shaker homes built up in strength and membership.

They made one great concession when they agreed to be photographed both in their homes and in the world. Many of these photographs appear in the following sections. Confident that the image they presented was altogether favorable, they embarked upon this plan with characteristic thoroughness.

171 Trustees' House and Office at Hancock in the 1880's.

172 Trustees' House at Hancock around the turn of the century. It was remodeled along Victorian lines in 1895.

173 Sisters in front of the dairy at the Second, or South, Family in Enfield, New Hampshire.

174 Enfield, New Hampshire.

175 Elder George Clark in a one-horse shay drawn by "Major." Enfield, Connecticut.

176 Shakers posing outside the Trustees' Office at Harvard on a summer's day.

177 Sisters at Harvard, Massachusetts. Left to right, Ellen Green, Eliza Babbitt, Marsha Bullard, Margaret Eggleton, Anne Walker.

178 North Family, Mount Lebanon. Robert Valentine is at left with the rake and hoe. Catherine Allen is in the last row center, next to Anna White, co-author with Leila S. Taylor of a well-known history of the Shakers. Several years later, Sister Catherine Allen helped William Cathcart, director of the Western Reserve Historical Society in Cleveland, to collect Shaker material and also asked the other Societies to make material available to him. We are thus indebted to her foresight for the preservation of much of the Shaker heritage.

179 Elder Frederick Evans surrounded by members of Mount Lebanon's North Family.

180 A group posing in the back yard of the North Family, Mount Lebanon.

181 Sisters from Mount Lebanon at an outdoor service of some sort. The location is unknown.

182 The oldest and the youngest at Mount Lebanon. Rufus Crossman (1798–1891) and Dolly Saxon (1776–1884) appear here in the last year of Sister Dolly's life.

183 Mount Lebanon. South Family Shakers, left to right, Ann Charles, Katie Boyle, Polly Lewis, Robert Wagan. Wagan had much to do with building up and maintaining the chair industry.

184 Mount Lebanon sisters pose in one of their early automobiles. Brothers did the driving.

SHAKER SISTER'S READY FOR AN AUTO RIDE, MT. LEBANON, N. Y.

185 Two sisters from Mount Lebanon, Polly Lewis and Katie Boyle, posing in a studio.

186 Watervliet, New York. This village was unique among Shaker communities in its layout, which grouped the buildings around a central common. The meeting house is at right. Watervliet was the first Shaker society, but it achieved formal organization later than Mount Lebanon.

187 Watervliet, New York. George Lomas is at left and Sister Harriet Bullard is second from left in the back row.

188 Brothers at Watervliet, New York.

189 Elder Thomas Smith, left rear, with sisters in the Lower Canaan, New York, family. Canaan was about five miles from Mount Lebanon.

190 Enfield, Connecticut, sisters in front of the side door of the South Family dwelling.

191 Sisters on the steps of the dwelling at Canterbury, New Hampshire.

192 Sisters pose at the Canterbury Trustees' Office, which also served as the post office of the community.

193 South Union, Kentucky. The meeting house is at right and the Centre Family dwelling is across the road, at left.

194 South Union, Kentucky. A group posing south of the meeting house. Eldress Nancy Moore is seated in the front row, at the far right. Elder Hervey Eades is standing, fourth from right.

195 The North Family house at Pleasant Hill, Kentucky, taken from a stereographic view.

196 Professor William M. Linney, state geologist, standing at right, has just given a lecture to the Shakers at Pleasant Hill.

197 Shaker sisters out for a walk at Pleasant Hill.

198 Shaker sisters at Pleasant Hill.

199 One of the first buildings of the South Family at Watervliet, New York. Sitting on the porch are, left to right, Anna Case, Rosetta Hendrickson, George Duncan, and Mary F. Dahm.

200 North Family, Watervliet, New York. This photograph was taken with flash powder.

201 Group from the South Family, Mount Lebanon.

202 Sisters at Watervliet, New York, in a picture taken with flash powder.

203 Sister Phoebe Lane of the Mount Lebanon community. This early photograph is dated either 1860 or 1869.

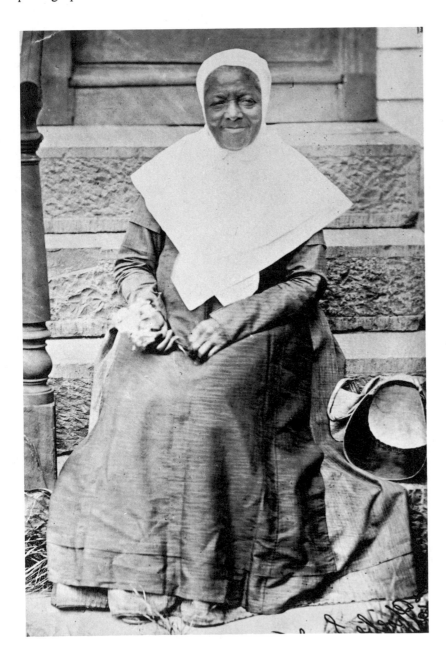

At Leisure

205 Canterbury sisters on an outing with young visitors wearing summer hats.

PRECEDING PAGE:
204 Pleasant Hill, Kentucky. Dr. William Pennebaker, left, and his brother, Dr. Francis Pennebaker, center, under a rustic wellhead behind the West Family house. Almost every Shaker village had a summerhouse or a shaded sitting room on the lawn.

Recreation and holidays were not considered superfluous or needless. Young and old alike entered into various programs to refresh mind and body. At Canterbury, the girls had gymnastic exercises and a flower garden. The boys played ball and marbles, went fishing, and had a small farm of their own.

Every community delighted in picnics, hayrides, berrying parties, sleigh rides, and excursions into the vast forests, which produced butternuts, walnuts, hickory nuts, and chestnuts. Community efforts in maple-sugaring and wood-chopping were festive occasions.

Hervey Elkins's account of his boyhood at Enfield, New Hampshire, tells of interesting companions, mild paternal control, and normal healthful experiences in a beautiful countryside where pleasant trips were frequently arranged.

The older Shakers took pleasure trips to the mountains, to the seashore, and to big cities where they visited cathedrals, museums, and national monuments.

The ministry in each society was obliged to visit every other society during the course of each year. Upon their return from a lengthy tour, it was customary for them to report in detail, often by reading the daily journal kept during the trip. In this way the brethren and the future elders and eldresses were put in touch with "the world," and at the same time the travelogue was a diversion.

206 Enfield, New Hampshire. Sisters of the South Family ready for a ride in the family four-seat platform wagon. Note the carriage-landing to help the sisters board the high cart.

207 William Briggs at Tebbits Pond, Canterbury, New Hampshire.

208 Boys at Canterbury, New Hampshire, posing and eating apples beside one of the eight man-made ponds which provided waterpower for the Shaker village.

209 Visiting another society.
Alfred, Maine, and Mount
Lebanon ministries, left to right:
Daniel Offord, Elder Otis
Sawyer, Eldress Hester Adams,
and Mary Ann Gillispie.
Standing are Margaret Patterson
and Eldress Anna White.

210 Group of Shakers from
Alfred, Maine, visiting Old
Orchard Beach. Prudence
Stickney is the young girl in the
foreground.

211 Mount Lebanon, New York. Elder Frederick W. Evans takes two eldresses, Antoinette Doolittle and Anna White, for a carriage ride on a sunny afternoon. The handsome meeting house, the second to be built at Mount Lebanon, was completed in 1824.

212 Alfred, Maine, dwelling and office. Shakers with their Pierce-Arrow, the first car owned by the society, at the start of a trip.

213 Sabbathday Lake, Maine. Brother Delmer Wilson at the wheel of the first car owned by that society, 1910.

182

214 Sabbathday Lake, Maine. Sisters taking off in their 1919 Pierce-Arrow. The sister behind the wheel was probably posing, although later many sisters learned to drive the family automobiles.

215 Canterbury ministry leaving Sabbathday Lake for home, June 5, 1916. Elder Arthur Bruce is the passenger in the front seat.

216 Mount Lebanon, New York. The North Family on an outing in a picnic grove. There was no racial discrimination among Shakers. Membership included American Indians, Europeans, and many Slavic peoples.

217 Watervliet Shakers on a trip.

218 Sisters playing croquet at Mount Lebanon, New York.

219 Shaker sisters at Canterbury singing for the Farmers' Exchange group in 1919.

From the first a special gift of harmony has seemed to rest upon the Canterbury society and many of the most refined and soul thrilling of the Shaker hymns have emanated from there.

—White and Taylor

220 Pleasànt Hill, Kentucky. Along the Kentucky River palisades, Shakers watch a photographer at work. The Believers used the river, on the edge of their property, for transporting their products and also maintained a ferry across it.

List of Stereographic Views

The following sets of stereographic views which are known to exist are in some instances entirely of Shaker subjects, but in others include only a few views of Shaker subjects. They are arranged according to the Shaker societies they depict and numbered for convenient reference.

CANTERBURY, N.H.

1. "Shaker Village, Canterbury, N.H." 22 views. Photographed and Published by W. G. C. Kimball, Concord, N.H.
2. Same as 1, 23 views.
3. Same as 1, 32 views.
4. "Photographic Views, Shaker Village, Canterbury, N.H." 58 views. W. G. C. Kimball, Photographer, Concord, N.H.
5. "Views of Concord and Vicinity, by H. A. Kimball, Concord, N.H." 127 mostly non-Shaker views.

ENFIELD, CONN.

6. "Views of Shaker Village of Enfield, Conn." 21 views. Goldsmith & Lazelle, Landscape & Portrait Photographers. Studio: Goodrich Block Main Street, near the Depot, Springfield, Mass.

ENFIELD, N.H.

7. "E. T. Brigham, Lebanon, N.H."
8. "Photographic Views, Shaker Village, Enfield, N.H." 24 views.
9. "From C. E. Lewis Gallery, Lebanon, N.H." 19 views.
10. "From C. E. Lewis Photographer, Lebanon, N.H." Rubber stamp on reverse.

HANCOCK, MASS.

11. Views exist, number and photographer unknown.

HARVARD, MASS.

12. Views exist, number and photographer unknown.

MOUNT LEBANON, N.Y.

13. "Photographs of Shaker Village, Mt. Lebanon, Columbia Co., N.Y." 27 views. A. J. Alden, Photographer, Pittsfield, Mass.
14. "Berkshire Series, Pittsfield and Vicinity." 48 views, of which 3 are Shaker. Published and for sale at wholesale and retail. William Nugend Variety Store, 55 North Street, Pittsfield, Mass.

15. "Shaker Village, Mt. Lebanon, N.Y." Irving, Photographer, Troy.
16. "Shaker Village, Mt. Lebanon." Irving, Photographer, 13 Second St., Troy, N.Y.
17. "Saratoga Springs and New Lebanon Shakers." McDonald & Sterry, Photographers, Albany and Saratoga Springs, N.Y. Some Shaker views, but mostly views of Saratoga Springs.

NORTH UNION, OHIO

18. Views exist, number and photographer unknown.

PLEASANT HILL, KY.

19. "Views of High Bridge, Ky. and Vicinity." 22 views, of which 10 are Shaker. Caldwell the Artist. "Aresto."
20. "Pleasant Hill Views." 8 views. Edward H. Fox, Artist, over Welch & Co., Danville, Ky.
21. "Views of the Kentucky River Bridge and Vicinity." A view of the Shaker ferry is the only Shaker subject among 20 views. Photographed and published by Edward H. Fox, Artist, Danville, Ky.
22. "Views of the Kentucky River Bridge and Vicinity." Same as 21. Photographed and Published by Edward H. Fox, Artist, over Welch & Wiseman's store. Danville, Ky.

SHIRLEY, MASS.

23. "Views of Shirley." B. F. Foster, South Street, Milford, N.H.
24. "Shaker Village & Scenery, in Shirley, Middlesex County, Mass. Taken in the Summer of 1871." Photographed by J. C. Moulton, Fitchburg, Mass.

TYRINGHAM, MASS.

25. Published by E. A. Morley, East Lee, Mass.

WATERVLIET, N.Y.

26. Irving Photographer, Troy, N.Y.
27. "Shaker Village." Irving Photographer, Troy.
28. Clark Photographer, Pittsfield, Mass.

Bibliography

MANUSCRIPTS

Bates, Issachar. Sketch: the Life and Experience of Issachar Bates (copy by Betsy Smith).

Journal A (1804–1836) Kept at South Union by H. L. Eades. Contains autobiography of John Rankin, Sr. (1746–1834) and a portion of a journal kept by B. S. Youngs at Busro.

Journal B (1837–1864) kept at South Union.

Journal C (1865–1871) kept at South Union.

Journal D (1879–1917) kept at South Union.

Journal 1871–1872 kept at South Union by Lucy Shannon.

Letter from Molly Goodrich, Union Village, Ohio, August 18, 1806, to the Beloved Sisters at New Lebanon (copy in South Union letter book).

PUBLICATIONS

Andrews, Edward Deming. *The People Called Shakers.* New York, Oxford University Press, 1953.

———. *The Community Industries of the Shakers.* Albany, The University of the State of New York, 1933.

Ashe, Thomas. *Travels in America.* New York, 1810.

Basting, Louis, "The Believers of Indiana in 1811," in *The Manifesto* XV. Jan. 1890.

Bernard, Duke of Saxe-Weimar-Eisenach. *Travels through North America, 1825–26.* Philadelphia, Carey, Lea, and Carey, 1828. Volume I.

Blaney, W. H. *Excursion through the United States and Canada, 1822–23.* London, 1824.

Blinn, Henry C. *Gentle Manners.* East Canterbury, N.H., The United Society, 1899. Third edition.

———. *In Memoriam.* Concord, N.H., 1905.

Bremer, Fredericka. *The Homes of the New World.* New York, Harper & Bros., 1853.

Buckingham, D. A. "Epitomic History of the Watervliet Shakers," in *The Shaker* VII. May–Nov. 1877.

Carll, Anna P. "Reminiscences of My Shaker Childhood," in *The Manifesto* XVII. Feb.–May 1887.

Cist's Weekly Advertiser. July 26, 1848.

Colin, Mary Lou. *The North Union Story.* Shaker Heights, 1961.

Daubenny, Charles. *Journal of a Tour through the United States and Canada.* Oxford, 1843.

Dixon, W. Hepworth. *New America.* Philadelphia, J. B. Lippincott & Co., 1867.

Elam, Aida. *History of the Shakers.* Canterbury, n.d.

Elkins, Hervey. *Fifteen Years in the Senior Order of the Shakers.* Hanover, Dartmouth Press, 1853.

Evans, Frederick W. *Autobiography of a Shaker.* New York, American News Co., 1888.

Finch, Marianne. *An Englishwoman's Experience in America.* London, R. Bentley, 1833.

Frost, Marguerite. *About the Shakers.* Canterbury, 1958.

———. *The Shaker Story.* Canterbury, n.d.

Gardener's Manual, The. New Lebanon, 1843.

Greeley, Horace. "A Sabbath with the Shakers," in *The Knickerbocker* XI. June 1838.

Greene, Nancy Lewis. *Ye Olde Shaker Bells.* Lexington, Ky., 1930.

Greylock, Godfrey (Smith, J. E. A.). *Taghconic, or Letters and Legends.* Boston, 1852.

Hinds, William Alfred. *American Communities.* Oneida, N.Y., Office of the American Socialist, 1878.

"History of the Church of Mount Lebanon, N.Y.," in *The Manifesto* XIX, July 1889, and XX, October 1890.

Hutton, Daniel M. *Old Shakertown and the Shakers.* Harrodsburg, Ky., 1936.

Janson, C. W. *Stranger in America.* London, 1807.

Johnson, Theodore E., editor. *The Shaker Quarterly.* Poland Spring, Maine, 1961–73.

Kaiandre, Theo. "Christian Communism," reprinted from The Cincinnati *Post* in *The Manifesto* XVII, April–July 1887.

King, Emma B. *A Shaker's Viewpoint.* Chatham, N.Y., 1967.

Letter to *The Manifesto* from South Union, March 1891.

Letter to *The Manifesto* from South Union, April 1891.

Lindsey, Bertha. *Industries and Inventions.* Canterbury, n.d.

MacLean, J. P. *The Shakers of Ohio. Fugitive Papers.* Columbus, 1907.

Marryat, Capt. Frederick. *Diary in America.* London, Longman, Orme, Brown, Green & Longman, 1839. Volume I.

Martineau, Harriet. *Society in America.* London, Saunders & Otley, 1837. Volume II.

McClelland, Samuel D. "Busro," in *The Manifesto* XV, May–Sept. 1885.

Melcher, Marguerite. *The Shaker Adventure.* Princeton, Princeton University Press, 1941.

Messerli, Jonathan. *Horace Mann, A Biography.* New York, Alfred A. Knopf, 1972.

Murray, Amelia. *Letters from the United States, Cuba, and Canada.* New York, G. P. Putnam & Co., 1856.

Neal, Julia. *By Their Fruits.* Chapel Hill, University of North Carolina Press, 1947.

———, ed. *The Journal of Eldress Nancy.* Nashville, Parthenon Press, 1963.

Nordhoff, Charles. *The Communistic Societies of the United States.* New York, Harper & Brothers, 1875.

Noyes, John Humphrey. *A History of American Socialisms.* Philadelphia, 1870.

Palmer, John. *Journal of Travels in the United States and Lower Canada.* London, 1817.

Peculiarities of the Shakers, by a Visitor (Benjamin Silliman of Yale). New York, 1832.

Phelps, Lillian. "Reminiscences of Shaker Recreational Life," in *The Shaker Quarterly.* Summer 1961.

Piercy, Caroline B. *The Valley of God's Pleasure.* New York, Stratford House, 1951.

Pittsfield *Sun,* The. "Shakers at Pittsfield, Mass." August 14, 1834.

Precepts of Mother Ann Lee and the Elders. Albany, 1888.

Purtell, Joseph. *The Tiffany Touch.* New York, Random House, 1971.

Rathbun, Valentine. *Brief Hints of a Religious Scheme.* Norwich, 1781.

Robb, Marywebb Gibson. *Shakerism in Kentucky.* Lexington, 1942.

Ross, James. *Life and Times of Elder Reuben Ross.* Philadelphia, n.d.

Sears, Clara Endicott. *Gleanings from Old Shaker Journals.* Boston and New York, Houghton Mifflin Co., 1916.

"Shakers, The," by a correspondent for *The Penny Magazine.* London, Nov. 18, 1837.

Stuart, James. *Three Years in America.* Edinburgh, 1833. Volume I.

A Summary View of the Millennial Church. Albany, Packard and Van Benthuysen, 1823.

Swem, E. G., ed. *Letters on Kentucky, 1825.* Reprinted from The Richmond [Ky.] *Enquirer,* Apr.–May 1825. New York, Heartman's Historical Series, printed for C. F. Heartman, 1916.

Taylor, Amos. *Narrative of the Strange Principles, Conduct, and Character of the People Known by the Name of Shakers.* Worcester, Mass., 1782.

Taylor, Leila S. *A Memorial to Eldress Anna White and Elder Daniel Offord.* Mount Lebanon, The North Family, 1912.

Thomas, S. W. and Thomas, J. C. *The Simple Spirit.* Pleasant Hill, The Pleasant Hill Press, 1973.

Wall, Miriam. *Education and Recreation.* Canterbury, n.d.

Whitcher, Mary. *Mary Whitcher's Shaker House-Keeper.* Canterbury, 1882.

White, Anna. *Immortalized: Elder Frederick W. Evans.* Pittsfield, 1893.

White, Anna and Taylor, Leila S. *Shakerism: Its Meaning and Message.* Columbus, 1904.

Willis, Nathaniel Parker. *Health Trip to the Tropics.* New York, C. Scribner, 1854.